PELHAM HUMFREY

Oxford Studies of Composers (21)

PELHAM HUMFREY

PETER DENNISON

Oxford   New York

OXFORD UNIVERSITY PRESS

1986

Oxford University Press, Walton Street, Oxford OX2 6DP

Oxford New York Toronto
Delhi Bombay Calcutta Madras Karachi
Petaling Jaya Singapore Hong Kong Tokyo
Nairobi Dar es Salaam Cape Town
Melbourne Auckland

and associated companies in
Beirut Berlin Ibadan Nicosia

Oxford is a trade mark of Oxford University Press

Published in the United States
by Oxford University Press, New York

British Library Cataloguing in Publication Data
Dennison, Peter
Pelham Humfrey.—(Oxford studies of composers)
1. Humfrey, Pelham—Criticism and interpretation
I. Title
780'.92'4   ML410.H/
ISBN 0-19-315244-4
ISBN 0-19-315234-7 Pbk

Library of Congress Cataloging in Publication Data
Dennison, Peter, 1942–
Pelham Humfrey.
(Oxford studies of composers; 21)
Bibliography: p.
Includes index.
1. Humfrey, Pelham, 1647–1674.   2. Composers—
England—Biography.   I. Title.   II. Series: Oxford
studies of composers; 21.
ML410.H929D4   1986   780'.92'4 [B]   86–12765
ISBN 0-19-315244-4
ISBN 0-19-315234-7 (pbk.)

Set by Latimer Trend & Co Ltd, Plymouth
Printed in Great Britain by
Richard Clay (The Chaucer Press) Ltd,
Bungay, Suffolk

CONTENTS

for Stephen

ABBREVIATIONS

Voices: Lower case = soloists, tr, a, t, b; upper case = tutti, Tr, A, T, B
Instruments: vn = violin, va = viola, bc = basso continuo
t-s = time signature

(16)   refers to work number 16 in the List of Works
(4.56) refers to work number 4 in the List of Works, bar 56

References to manuscript sources are by means of RISM sigla where, for example, *GB-Lbl* means Great Britain, London, British Library

I

PELHAM HUMFREY, CHILD OF THE RESTORATION

THE restoration of Charles II to the English throne in May 1660 initiated a new era of creativity in both the arts and sciences. Those who invited Charles to return were weary of puritan rule and eager to establish a system of government under a monarchy tempered by the will of Parliament. On his return Charles was given an overwhelming welcome by the populace in Dover, Canterbury, and London, and he was enthusiastically acclaimed as head of state and society by the leaders of the nation. In affairs of state he wielded his authority with caution, but in society he quickly became a dictator of fashion and an arbiter of taste. As a result of his experiences abroad his tastes were decidedly French.

Charles had left an increasingly hostile England in 1646 and joined his mother, Henrietta Maria, at the French court at the Louvre, where both remained until 1654. Charles's arrival had been celebrated at court by spectacular entertainments of *ballets* and *comédies*, and both he and his mother regularly participated in the lavish Italianate spectacles then in vogue. No sooner had he returned to England than Charles sought to surround himself with music, both sacred and secular, of comparable magnificence. His most immediate models were French, and their promotion in his secular household is confirmed by Roger North (*c.*1651–1734), who, although writing as late as 1728, was probably reflecting the eyewitness account of his teacher, John Jenkins:

... during the first years of Charles II all musick affected by the *beau-mond* run into the French way; ... King Charles II was a professed lover of musick, but of this kind onely. . .[1]

As early as 1660 Charles had a consort of French musicians, and in 1666 he appointed the Frenchman Louis Grabu Master of the King's Musick, the foremost musical position at court. During the first decade of his reign, he sent two musicians, John Banister and Pelham Humfrey, to Paris to absorb at first hand the styles that he had so admired during his exile, and that he now sought to introduce to his not always enthusiastic English subjects.

Violinists were appointed to the Royal household from June 1660, and by the end of the year Matthew Locke and the elder Henry Purcell were two of four composers appointed specifically for the violin. Early in 1661 these players became the King's band of Twenty-four Violins, and they were first heard in public on 22 April at the entertainments on the eve of Charles's coronation, and at the coronation itself. At the festivities in Westminster Hall after the coronation, Samuel Pepys 'took a great deal of pleasure ... to hear the Musique of all sorts; but above all, the 24 viollins'.[2] Charles's Twenty-four were modelled directly on the *Vingt-Quatre Violons du Roy* that were rising to new heights of excellence during his years of exile at the French court. In 1652 Lully joined the band, and the next year collaborated in the composition of his first *ballet*. Lully's rise was rapid, and in 1656 he was given his own band to train, the *Troupe des petits Violons*, a select group of sixteen players which was later increased to twenty-one. During the ensuing decades, Lully developed in these bands a style of ensemble string playing that was renowned for its precision of intonation and rhythm, and, in the words of Georg Muffat, for 'a sweetness, vigor, and beauty ... distinguishing it from [other styles]'.[3]

John Banister the elder was appointed a violinist in the Royal household in 1660, and was among the Twenty-four Violins from the start. On 2 December 1661 he was given leave 'to go into France on special service, and return with expedition',[4] and this could only have been to undertake a study of French styles of string playing and composition. He had returned by the following March, and on 3 May 1662 was given

full power to instruct and direct twelve persons ... chosen by him out of the twenty-four of the band of violins, for better performance of service, without being mixed with the other violins, unless when the King orders the twenty-four.[5]

The idea of a select band of twelve must have been Banister's in direct imitation of Lully's *Petits Violons* which was formed after Charles had left the French court.

In the preface to his *Florilegium Secundum* (1698), Georg Muffat specifically testified that Lully's style was practised by the English.[6] Muffat had studied under Lully in Paris between 1663 and 1669, and may well have heard of English practice from one of the English visitors in Paris in those years. There is ample evidence in contemporary English treatises[7] that from this time Lully's 'rule of the down bow' and his ensemble precision were becoming increasingly known and emulated among English violinists.

The heart of the Royal musical household was the Chapel Royal, and every important court musician was connected with it in some way. Nowhere were the stimulus of the King and his preference for new styles more decisive. Writing in 1716, Thomas Tudway, one of the first set of choristers, ascribed the innovations in the Chapel to this 'brisk, & Airy Prince' who was soon 'tyr'd with the Grave & Solemn way, And Order'd the Composers of his Chappell, to add Symphonys &c with Instruments to their Anthems'.[8] The restoration of the Chapel music was entrusted to the indefatigable and colourful Captain Henry Cooke. He was born about 1615, became a chorister in the Chapel Royal of Charles I, and was appointed Master of the Children of the Chapel Royal about the middle of 1660. Services in the Chapel Royal of Charles I had been suspended in 1644, and Cooke had to build the boys' section of his choir after a break in continuity of sixteen years. He began recruiting immediately and even revived the practice of pressing boys into service from choral foundations in the country. Cooke had his full complement of twelve boys well before the end of 1660, and his unfailing skill in selecting real talent and the excellence of his training are proved by the fact that well over half of the first set of boys emerged as the leaders of the next generation of English musicians. These included Pelham Humfrey, John Blow, Michael Wise, William Turner, and Thomas Tudway; the great Henry Purcell became a boy chorister probably about the end of the decade. The best of Cooke's boys not only sang but also composed as Tudway recollected:

... some of the forwardest, & brightest Children of the Chappell, as Mr Humfreys, Mr Blow, &c, began to be Masters of a faculty in Composing; This, his Majesty greatly encourag'd, by indulging their youthfull fancys, so that ev'ry Month at least, & afterwards oft'ner, they produc'd something New, of this Kind; In a few years more, Severall others, Educated in the Chappell, produc'd their Compositions in this Style, for otherwise, it was in vain to hope to please his Majesty.[9]

Unlike the boys' section of the Choir, the appointment of Gentlemen of the Chapel Royal was able to draw on some continuity from the past as at least six of the first singers had been members of the Chapel of Charles I. Some of the Gentlemen were singing by July 1660, and by the time of the coronation they were up to their full strength of thirty-two. Of these there were initially sixteen basses, and eight each of tenors and countertenors, although except on special occasions the Gentlemen rotated on a monthly roster system. In 1671 the thirty-two were reduced to twenty-four, eight of each part, and these too rotated monthly. From the Gentlemen were selected a Master of the Children of the Chapel Royal, and three who served as organists.

The Twenty-four Violins first played with the Chapel Royal Choir at the coronation in April 1661, but from September 1662 the band, or more likely part of it, was introduced into the regular service of the Chapel when the King attended, that is on Sunday mornings and on holy days.[10] On 14 September 1662, Pepys noted 'the first day of having Vialls [sc. violins] and other Instruments to play a Symphony between every verse of the Anthem', and on 21 December 1662 John Evelyn complained that

instead of the antient grave and solemn wind musique accompanying the *Organ* was introduced a Consort of 24 Violins betweene every pause, after the *French* fantastical light way, better suiting a Tavern or Play-house than a Church.

The group that played in Chapel initially was probably the twelve which Banister had selected the previous May, but in November 1671 a monthly rota was drawn up consisting of three groups of five players each. This must have been inadequate as only four months later each group was increased to six players.[11]

The services of the Chapel Royal in which the most elaborate musical resources were concentrated were those which the King himself attended, and the principal musical item was the anthem. In the first year or so of the Restoration, the repertory of the Chapel was based almost exclusively on anthems sung before the Civil War. The book of anthem texts used in the Chapel dating from about 1663[12] reproduced the book used in the Chapel about 1635[13] with the addition of four full anthems and twenty-five verse anthems, most dating from the first years of the Restoration. The second edition of James Clifford's *The Divine Services and Anthems* (1664) was intended to supersede this, and contains the first indication of a significant body of post-Restoration anthems sung in the Chapel. These are primarily verse anthems with a predominance of solo voices, alone and in ensemble, and many with sections for strings. They include twenty by Cooke, four by

4

Locke, and no fewer than fourteen by three Children of the Chapel: five by Pelham Humfrey, three by John Blow, and six by Robert Smith. Of the fourteen, only Humfrey's *Haste thee O God* has survived. A list of services and anthems transcribed into the Chapel Royal part books between 1670 and 1676[14] confirms the predominance of the newer style in the second decade of the Restoration during the successive Masterships of Cooke, Humfrey, and Blow. The bulk of these anthems are by Gentlemen of the Chapel including nine each by Blow and Child, six by Humfrey, three by Turner, and eleven each by Wise and Tucker. These lists testify that by fifteen years after the Restoration the newer styles and techniques which had been so actively encouraged by the King and eagerly pursued by his musicians had become firmly established. Thus the baroque styles which had been flourishing in some European centres for well over half a century were finally coming of age in a country that, although on the artistic periphery of Europe, could react positively to the impetus that was provided by the cosmopolitan Charles II.

This environment offered ideal opportunities for nurturing prodigious musical talent, and just such a talent appeared in the earliest months of the Restoration in the person of Pelham Humfrey. At the age of twelve or thirteen, he became one of Captain Cooke's first and most precocious choristers, and in the next decade and a half he in his turn, as composer, performer, and musical leader, left that environment richer musically than he had found it. From the epitaph on his tomb, which had become obliterated after only a century,[15] it can be deduced that Humfrey had been born between 15 July 1647 and 13 July 1648. Burney opted for 1647, although as Humfrey's voice broke at about the same time as Blow's (both boys left the Choir for this reason at Christmas 1664) and Blow was born in February 1649, Humfrey may have been born in 1648 rather than 1647. The evidence, however, is circumstantial at best. The contemporary gossip Anthony à Wood identified Pelham as the nephew of Colonel John Humfrey, a prominent Cromwellian and resident of London during the Civil War and Commonwealth. Pelham may thus have been a native of London himself; there is no suggestion that he was among those pressed into the Chapel Royal Choir from the country.

Humfrey may well have been in the Choir by mid-1660, and he appears to have been the most conspicuously talented of the early

5

choristers. On 22 November 1663 Pepys noted in his diary that 'the Anthemne was good after the sermon, being the 51 psalme—made for five voices by one of Captain Cookes boys, a pretty boy'. The only known anthem that fits this description is the first working of *Have mercy upon me O God* by Humfrey. In 1664 the texts of no fewer than five of his anthems were published in the second edition of Clifford's *The Divine Services and Anthems*. While still a boy he also collaborated with two fellow choristers, Turner and Blow, in the so-called 'Club' anthem, *I will always give thanks*, which was composed, as Boyce explained in 1773, 'to remain as a memorial of their fraternal esteem and friendship'.[16]

When a boy left the Choir, Cooke was customarily paid £30 for his upkeep, and indeed this sum was ratified retrospectively on 17 May 1665 for two boys including Blow who, with Humfrey, had left the Choir on Christmas Day 1664. In the same warrant, however, Cooke was paid £40 for the upkeep of Humfrey, indicating no doubt the pre-eminent position Humfrey had attained as a composer among the choristers by that stage. His potential was rewarded yet further immediately after he left the Choir, and before the end of 1664 he was given £200 from Secret Service funds 'to defray the charge of his journey into France and Italy'.[17] In 1665 he received a further £100, and in 1666 £150 from the same source. The purpose of his travels can only have been to study at first hand the latest styles and techniques of composition in France and Italy. There is no contemporary account of Humfrey's experiences abroad. The only direct evidence lies in the music that he wrote after his return, and this strongly suggests a close knowledge of the music of Lully, and of Italians such as Carissimi. About a century later, Boyce, who may have had access to evidence now lost, wrote that Humfrey was sent to France 'to receive further Instruction from *John Baptist Lully*, a *Florentine* Musician of great Eminence, at that Time in the Service of the *French* Court'.[18] Lully accepted Muffat as a pupil between 1663 and 1669, and it is not unlikely that he would have accepted Humfrey also, particularly as the latter was sent by Charles II, who was no longer a poor relation of Louis XIV. In all probability Humfrey met the young Muffat in Paris.

During his absence, Humfrey was appointed a musician for the lute in the private music, the King's chamber music, on 10 March 1666, and on 24 January 1667 he was appointed a Gentleman of the Chapel Royal. He arrived back in England in October 1667 with the world at his feet, and the court eagerly awaiting a display of his art. He was sworn into his place as a Gentleman on 26 October, and is known to have sung tenor. On 1 November following, All Saints' Day, an anthem composed by him in France pending his return was performed in the Chapel. Pepys seems to have been taken by surprise, and recorded

a fine Anthemne, made by Pellam (who is come over) in France, of which there was great expectation; and endeed is a very good piece of Musique, but still I cannot call the Anthem anything but Instrumentall music with the Voice, for nothing is made of the words at all.

The proportion of instrumental involvement was probably greater than Pepys was expecting, and must have diverted his attention from Humfrey's finely calculated word setting. Pepys adjusted to the new style, however, and on 29 May 1669, two days before his Diary ceases, he was able to report 'a good anthem of Pelham's'.

The fullest contemporary descriptions of Humfrey's music and character come from Pepys, and in the first weeks of Humfrey's return, Pepys developed a strong antipathy to Humfrey's vanity. On 15 November 1667 his exasperation reached its height.

Thence I away home (calling at my Mercer and tailor's) and there find, as I expected, Mr. Caesar [Duffill] and little Pellam Humphrys, lately returned from France and is an absolute Monsieur, as full of form and confidence and vanity, and disparages everything and everybody's skill but his own. The truth is, everybody says he is very able; but to hear how he laughs at all the King's music here, as Blagrave and others, that they cannot keep time nor tune nor understand anything, and that Grebus the Frenchman, the King's Master of the Musique, how he understands nothing nor can play on any instrument and so cannot compose, and that he will give him a lift out of his place, and that he and the King are mighty great, and that he hath already spoke to the King of Grebus, would make a man piss.

Humfrey's extravagant assertions may well have been in response to what could have seemed Pepys's staid attitude, but some of them do specifically reflect his French experiences. His accusation that English players could keep neither 'time nor tune' would seem to have been directly influenced by Lully's discipline as these qualities, *tempus* and *contactus*, are two of the five categories under which Muffat was later to summarize Lully's style.[19]

Humfrey's bumptiousness originated probably at a formative stage as an identification with the flamboyant behaviour of Captain

7

Cooke, and as a result of the attention that his precocity earned him. It must have been reinforced by a need to compensate for his small stature, and finally consolidated by the likely desire to assume at the English court the same influence as Lully was beginning to wield in Paris. After the initial impact of his return, however, Humfrey's first four years back in England were relatively uneventful. He would regularly have composed anthems for the Chapel, served as a lutenist in the private music, and composed songs for court and domestic use, and for the theatre. On 21 January 1670 he was elected one of the assistants of the Corporation of Music, the musicians' guild that was particularly active during his lifetime.

In contrast to these early years, the last two and a half years of Humfrey's life saw his rise to the foremost musical positions at court, and to his becoming one of the most prominent musicians in the city. The flood of activity began with his being invited to set the court ode for New Year's Day 1672. *See mighty Sir* must have met with Royal approval as only ten days later Humfrey was appointed a composer for the violins jointly with Thomas Purcell, and he was entrusted with providing the ode for the King's birthday, *When from his Throne*, on 29 May following.

Some time in the second half of 1672, Humfrey married Katherine Cooke, the daughter of his old master. The occasion was celebrated by Humfrey's friend and the author of these two court odes, Robert Veel (1648–?74), with *An Hymeneal to my Dear Friend Mr. P. H.*.[20] Amid the conventional metaphors, the only possible glimpse of the personality of the composer lies in Veel's addressing him as 'Jolly Youth'. A daughter was christened Mary at St Margaret's Church Westminster on 21 November 1673, but she died three months later, and was buried on 23 February 1674.

Humfrey was elected one of the annual Wardens of the Corporation of Music on 24 June 1672. The aged Henry Cooke died on 13 July 1672, and the following day Humfrey succeeded him as Master of the Children of the Chapel Royal and a composer in the private music,[21] thus becoming the foremost musician at court. As Master of the Children, Humfrey taught the boys not only singing, but also the violin, lute, and theorbo,[22] and probably taught his brightest choristers composition. Foremost of these was Henry Purcell who remained a chorister under Humfrey until 29 September 1673.[23] To the demands of his positions at court was added in the final months of his life the composition of two substantial masques and a song for Shadwell's spectacular new production of *The Tempest*. This Opera, as contemporary commentators described it, became an equally grand musical collaboration between Humfrey, Locke, Reggio, and probably Draghi. The cast included some of the men and boys from the Chapel, and a section of the Twenty-four Violins, and Humfrey was probably involved in the production which opened about 30 April 1674.

Humfrey did not travel to Windsor with the court that year for the St George's Day celebrations, and this may have been because of ill health, or preparations for *The Tempest*, or both. On the very day, 23 April 1674, he made his will, and it was witnessed by Blow.[24] The court returned to Windsor for the summer on 18 May following, and Humfrey did accompany them this time. While there, however, on Tuesday 14 July and after a weekend of French entertainments, he died. He was buried in the cloisters of Westminster Abbey near the south-east door on 17 July, and his epitaph bore the inscription 'Here lieth interred the body of Mr. *Pelham Humphrey*, who died the fourteenth of *July*, *Anno Dom.* 1674. and in the twenty seventh year of his age.'[25] His will was proved on 30 July following.

Humfrey's former colleague in the private music, the younger William Gregory, set a *Pastoral Song . . . in memory of his deceased Friend Mr. Pelham Humphrys*,[26] and its poem, by Flatman, testified to the power of Humfrey's art, and the esteem in which it was held. Decades later, in a dedicatory poem addressing Purcell posthumously and published in the third edition of *Orpheus Britannicus*, Henry Hall, a former chorister of Humfrey, remembered his old master's contribution as he traced the progress of the muse of music from Italy, through France, and finally to England:

> Where with young *Humphries* she acquainted grew,
> (Our first reforming Music's *Richelieu*)
> Who dying left the Goddess all to You.[27]

Humfrey was a child of the new age, and he did perhaps more than any other composer in the first fifteen years of the Restoration to consolidate the newer styles of the baroque, and to bring them to a belated maturity in England. He was unreservedly committed to these styles and to the aesthetic that lay behind them, and went on to express the spirit of the age in an output that was both distinctive and distinguished. In so doing, Humfrey made perhaps the most significant musical contribution of his day to Charles II's vision of an English court as opulent and modish as any in Europe.

TOWARDS AN ENGLISH BAROQUE

THE baroque aesthetic, which shaped the English artistic climate from the beginning of the Restoration, exaggerated the humanism of the late Renaissance, and sought an ever more vivid and disturbing expression of human emotions and their fluctuations. To its contemporaries, it contrasted decisively with the values of the previous age, and Roger North, writing about 1726 but reflecting on the England of his formative years, clarified the essential distinctions as he saw them in the case of music.

Musick hath 2 ends. First to please the sence, and that is done by the pure Dulcor of Harmony, which is found cheifly in the elder musick, ... And secondly to move the affections, or excite passion.[1]

North's second end had originated in Italy about the beginning of the seventeenth century where it gave birth to a second practice of music, the *seconda prattica*. Consolidated in the work of Monteverdi, this became the basis of the Italian style for much of the century. It began essentially as a secular vocal style where emotional immediacy was achieved through finely calculated melodic angularity, chromatic and unexpected harmony, and a passionate manner of singing. Soon, however, it permeated and transformed sacred forms like the motet with a more emotive and declamatory setting of words, and with a bass line that infused into these traditional textures a new harmonic momentum.

Perhaps the single most influential Italian composer in England after the Restoration was Iacomo Carissimi (1605–74). His pupil Vicenzo Albrici was active in London in the 1660s, manuscripts of his motets and cantatas circulated in England in the second half of the century, and it is possible that Pelham Humfrey encountered him during his three years abroad 1665–7. Carissimi's style embodies the essentials of the *seconda prattica* together with second generation modifications which he played a major part in evolving. Carissimi and his contemporaries adopted three principal vocal textures, the starkly declamatory recitative, duple in time and often built around arpeggio patterns, at one extreme, and at the other the lyrical, triple-time aria with a regular formal structure. To these they added the intermediate arioso customarily in duple time, but characterized both by a melodic flexibility ranging from the declamatory to the lyrical, and by a variable harmonic rhythm. The arioso could include measured musical elements such as sequences and coloratura, and it often established a close thematic integration between the melody and the bass. Above all its flexibilities of texture made it a particularly subtle medium for delineating complex fluctuations of emotion.

Carissimi grafted these new expressive idioms into his motets, many of which are scored for two or three voices and continuo, and these were particularly influential in England after the Restoration. In the final phrase of the motet *Hodie Simon Petrus* (Ex. 1) the heavy grief suggested by the text is reinforced by flat inflexions in the tenor lines and in the harmony. The repeated and consecutive seconds between the two tenors in bars 2–3 and 6–7 prior to the cadences were a particular imprint of the Italian style, and the sequential repetition of the first three-bar phrase from bar 5 illustrates the grafting of a newer harmonic technique into a traditional imitative texture. This motet was known in England after the Restoration, and one contemporary English source actually ascribes it to Henry Cooke.[2]

One of the most widely emulated of all Italian formal designs in both secular and sacred works was the bipartite vocal structure whose first section was in duple time and whose second was in triple time. The first was customarily declamatory in style with a slow rate of harmonic change, and the second was more lyrical, its melody often built around arpeggio patterns, and its rate of harmonic change faster. The essentials of this bipartite structure are found in a short episode from the motet *Filiae Jerusalem* by Antonio Cesti (1623–69) (Ex. 2). Works by Cesti including this motet were also known in Restoration England.

Some knowledge of Italian styles had filtered into England in the first half of the seventeenth century through foreign visitors, through Englishmen such as Dering and Porter who spent some time in Italy, and through the circulation of Italian music in England. However experiments 'after the Italian way'[3] in these years were on a modest scale and were cautious, lacking both the stimulus of a stable source of patronage, and, for the most part, composers capable of adapting the newer styles on any extensive scale to English conditions.

11

Ex. 1   Carissimi

GB - Lbl Egerton 2960, f. 79ᵛ

The most influential advocate of Italian baroque styles in the early years of the Restoration was Henry Cooke. Although his skills as a composer were limited, he was the most renowned and persuasive practitioner in England of the emotive techniques of singing that were equally fundamental to the style. As early as 1654 John Evelyn considered him 'the best singer after the *Italian* manner of any in *England*'.[4] In 1661 Pepys credited him with 'the best manner of singing in the world', and two years later identified him specifically with the Italian style of singing.[5] Into the 1664 edition of *A Brief Introduction To the Skill of Musick*, John Playford inserted an abridged translation of Caccini's Preface to *Le nuove musiche* (1602), itself symptomatic of a demand for a treatise on Italian vocal practice, and the art of gracing in particular. Playford added that this art had now achieved an 'Excellency and Perfection . . . by the Skill and furtherance of that Orpheus of our time *Henry Cook*'.[6] Pepys confirmed this skill when he wrote of Cooke's 'strange mastery . . . in making of extraordinary surprizing closes, that are mighty pretty', although on an earlier occasion before he had become accustomed to such embellishment, he had considered Cooke 'to overdo his part at singing'.[7]

As a composer, Cooke's most important contribution lay in his expansion of the verse anthem into a multi-sectional structure consisting of string preludes, verses, and choruses. In his hands the whole anthem revolved about the supremacy of singing by soloists, and that was the contribution of a singer. Though his own style of composition was disjointed and fragmentary, his format did provide a structural basis that was adopted and expanded by his greater successors. The string movements in Cooke's anthems, equally often in three or four parts, take as their models those of earlier English masque and theatre music with their strong dance associations: they show no evidence of any French influence. His opening movement, usually entitled prelude, is customarily independent of what follows, but the internal string movements are invariably related to adjacent vocal material after the Italian style. Cooke's anthems are dominated by their verses which are principally ensembles, and in these he assigned his most elaborate writing to the treble and bass voices. Within the verses there is a frequent alternation of duple- and triple-time sections, but this is only superficially Italianate: there is little stylistic distinction between sections, and the lyrical vein predominates. Cooke's choruses are of secondary importance, and often merely repeat material from the previous verse. His principal chorus usually

13

Ex. 2

Cesti

14

concludes the anthem, and internal choruses can be no more than punctuations of a few bars.

Although *Behold O God our defender*[8] was composed for the coronation in April 1661, its proportions are typical of Cooke's verse anthems with strings, and after the coronation it went into the repertory of the Chapel Royal where it would have been sung by Humfrey as a boy. The sectional analysis (Fig. 1) illustrates its construction from a large number of relatively short episodes. Of its thirteen sections, ten are fewer than twelve bars in length. The anthem lacks any calculated tonal design either between or within sections, and the recurrence of the 'alleluia' material reflects a poverty of invention rather than any planned unification. An

		scoring	bars	t-s	key	
1	Synfonye	a4	23	$\frac{4}{4}$	B flat	
2	Behold O God	tratb	24	$\frac{3}{4}$	B flat	
3	O how amiable	tratb	7	$\frac{4}{4}$	B flat	
4	O how amiable	TrATB	6	$\frac{4}{4}$	B flat	based on 3
5	Prelude	a4	8	$\frac{3}{4}$	B flat	anticipates 6
6	Alleluia	trb	10	$\frac{3}{4}$	B flat to F	Ex. 3
7	Alleluia	TrATB	3	$\frac{4}{4}$	F	Ex. 3
8	Ritornello	a4	2	$\frac{4}{4}$	F	Ex. 3
9	Alleluia	trb	11	$\frac{3}{4}$	F to C min	based on 6
10	Alleluia	TrATB	5	$\frac{4}{4}$	C min to B flat	related to 7
11	Ritornello	a4	2	$\frac{4}{4}$	B flat	
12	Alleluia	trb	18	$\frac{3}{4}$	B flat	based on 6
13	Alleluia	TrATB	5	$\frac{4}{4}$	B flat	

Total length: 124 bars

FIGURE 1　A Sectional Analysis of Cooke's anthem *Behold O God our defender*

Ex. 3

Cooke

GB - *Bu* 5001, f. 68

16

extract from within the anthem, sections 6, 7 and 8 (Ex. 3), illustrates Cooke's fragmentary invention, and in places his inept technique. Its harmonic basis is simple to the point of banality, but the writing for the treble and bass soloists shows a singer's understanding of the capacities of these voices. This extract gives some measure of the degree to which greater composers raised the basic prototype to an altogether higher artistry within the next decade.

The most significant English composer linking the Restoration with earlier Italian styles was Matthew Locke who in 1660 was aged 38. As early as 1648 he had copied 16 motets by minor Italians scored for one to three voices and continuo which he described as 'A Collection of Songs [made] when I was in the Low = Countreys 1648'.[9] In transcribing these motets, Locke gave himself a working knowledge of the style, and soon after he added to the same manuscript 14 English psalm settings and four Latin motets modelled on the style of his transcriptions. Throughout the 1650s his attraction to Italian vocal and dramatic conventions became stronger, and it found its most extensive application in *Cupid and Death* (1653) which blends these with those drawn from the English masque tradition.

Although he was never a Gentleman of the Chapel Royal, Locke wrote verse anthems for the Chapel after the Restoration, some ten of which are extant.[10] He adopted the multi-sectional structure and emphasis on verse singing of Cooke, but his anthems are of an altogether higher musical quality, structurally taut and eloquently expressive. They are nevertheless works of transition, and styles growing out of the late-Renaissance English anthem alternate, and are blended with more recent Italianate idioms. Perhaps the most distinctive characteristics of English music were an awareness of the expressive potential of chromatic harmony, and a natural inclination towards counterpoint. Locke's English ancestry is most apparent in his sustained contrapuntal writing for both strings and voices. In a number of his anthems there are sections in which a solo voice is joined by four imitative string parts that weave with the voice sustained five-part imitative polyphony. No other Restoration composer was so conspicuously indebted to the texture of the late-Renaissance anthem with viols. On the other hand Locke's melodic and harmonic idioms are saturated with the affecting language of the Italian baroque. His melodies abound in angular disjunct intervals, and his harmony confidently employs some of the most pungent dissonances of the day. Locke's string movements, usually entitled simphony or retornello, are customarily based on vocal material after the Italian manner, but he often develops that material imitatively, drawing on an older English tradition.

Locke's anthem *O be joyful in the Lord*,[11] scored for four-part strings, verse and chorus, was composed by 1664, and would have been sung by Humfrey as a boy. It is in the Anglo-Italianate style that he had been developing for at least a decade, yet its simphony shows some trace of the French elements that were to appear more prominently in his string writing after Humfrey had returned from abroad. The sectional analysis (Fig. 2) illustrates its overall structural similarity to Cooke's *Behold O God our defender* (Fig. 1) which is much the same length, and which dates from about the same time. Closer scrutiny, however, points to significant differences in the structural capacities of each composer. Locke's anthem is made up of ten sections, only four of which are fewer than twelve bars in length, and three of these are echoing ritornellos. All the string movements are built from vocal material, but none of the vocal sections duplicates other vocal material. Two verses, sections 2 and 6, are bipartite although neither follows the

		scoring	bars	t-s	key	
1	Simphony	a4	12	$\frac{3}{4}$	F	anticipates 2
2i	O be joyful	atb	10	$\frac{3}{4}$	F to C	
ii			4	$\frac{4}{4}$	C to F	
3	Simphony					repeats 1
4	Be sure	tr	9	$\frac{4}{4}$	F to D min	Ex. 4
5	Retornello	a4	3	$\frac{4}{4}$	D min	based on 4
6i	O go your way	atb	7	$\frac{4}{4}$	D min	
ii			15	$\frac{3}{4}$	D min to F	
7	Ritornello	a4	8	$\frac{3}{4}$	F	based on 6ii
8	For the Lord	tratb	22	$\frac{4}{4}$	D min to F	
9	Retornello	a4	4	$\frac{4}{4}$	F	based on 8
10	Glory be	TrATB, vns, va	26	$\frac{4}{4}$	B flat to F	

Total length (excluding 3): 120 bars

FIGURE 2   A Sectional Analysis of Locke's anthem *O be joyful in the Lord*

Italian prototype. All the ensembles have a high concentration of imitative counterpoint, a texture with which Locke was particularly fluent, and one that emphasizes his English lineage. The anthem has an overall tonal design with excursions from the pivotal F major, and its longer sections have an internal tonal organization with some move to a related key. Further unity is provided by a recurrence of the interval of the minor sixth which, falling in the bass and rising in the top part, pervades the anthem and is present in one or both forms in almost every section. This interval is a particular imprint of Locke's style as a whole, and contributes to the distinctiveness of his language. The particular species of motivic unity that it provides here was to be developed by Humfrey who found similar unification in the work of Lully. Locke's disjunct and even gaunt melodic style, which characterizes his solo, ensemble, and contrapuntal writing, is illustrated by the solo verse 'Be sure that the Lord', section 4 of this anthem (Ex. 4). There are rising minor sixths in the treble in bars 31, 33, and 35, and a falling minor sixth in the continuo in bar 31. The disjunct melody in the first half of bar 33 outlines the chord with a major third and a minor sixth which became a powerful expressive tool in the hands of the finest Restoration composers.

The Italian baroque style had its origins in vocal music, and in English music of the Restoration, it remained most influential on vocal music. Cooke and Locke were skilled in complementary aspects of the *seconda prattica*, and in the early years of the Restoration afforded England its most immediate contact with this style. They thus provided a vital antidote to the French bias which was being so actively promoted by the King.

The French style had its origins ironically in the Italian entertainments that Cardinal Mazarin had attempted to introduce to a reluctant French court in the 1640s and 1650s. In those years the astute young Lully aligned himself with the Italian faction, but after Mazarin's death in 1661 his truer strategy of displacing Italian fashion with a distinctly French musical style came to the fore unhampered by artistic or political expediency. The style that Lully created in the ensuing decades grew essentially out of the particular types of opera and ballet fostered at the French court. The most pervasively influential components of these, those which were imitated throughout Europe for at least a century, were their instrumental movements, *ouvertures*, *ritournelles*, and dances. These were written for the *Vingt-Quatre Violons du Roy* or the

sheep of his pas-ture.

Troupe des petits Violons, and occasioned a species of ensemble precision and virtuosity which were distinctly different from the solo-orientated textures of contemporary Italian music.

The form evolved by Lully which was most widely emulated in Restoration England was the French *ouverture*. One of his earliest, written in 1657 for the Prologue of the *ballet L'Amour Malade*,[12] falls into what became his customary bipartite form, but its second section was a triple-time homophonic movement adopting the idioms of the contemporary French sarabande rather than the fugal texture that he more usually adopted later (Ex. 5). It was this less common type together with many of its technical details that composers of the early Restoration period appropriated. Both duple and triple sections maintain a harmonic polarity, yet with some thematic integration between the outer parts, and although the writing is in five parts, the most usual number in Lully's *ouvertures*, interest is concentrated in the outer parts. These polarities can be traced back to the practice of the Italian arioso. The duple-time section does not yet possess any ordered tonal structure with internal cadences after the Italian manner; rather it achieves its continuity by the conspicuous avoidance of cadence, and by a resultant harmonic fluidity. Unity is provided by thematic concentration, here by the descending conjunct phrases that permeate the bass line, and consequently filter into the top part. Such unification by thematic rather than tonal means was beginning to distinguish the French from the Italian style even as early as this. The single-bar rhythmic pattern which dominates the triple section, ♩♩.♪ is a simpler version of the sarabande pattern ♩♩.♪ | ♩.♩♪ which Lully regularly employed, and which was widely used by English Restoration composers.

Elements of the French style could well have been introduced into England at the beginning of the Restoration by the King's consort of French musicians. The first Englishman to come into

Ex. 5

Lully

23

direct contact with Lully was John Banister, and the music he wrote after his return from France about March 1662 confirms the strength of that influence. A section of a two-part Ayre, one of twelve dances from *The Musick at the Bath* dating from the second half of 1663,[13] reflects the thematic integration between the outer parts and the harmonic fluidity found in Lully (Ex. 6). The opening of Banister's Braule in A minor (Ex. 7) is in the four parts more customary in English string music. It adopts Lully's concerted rhythmic precision and the idiom of the contemporary French courante, complete with its recurrent hemiola pattern $\frac{3}{4}$♩. ♪♪|♩♩.♪.Whatever Banister's limitations, he did provide the Restoration with its earliest immediate link with the French style, and furnished a model which greater composers were able to turn to more accomplished ends. Locke absorbed some elements of the style in the early 1660s, and Humfrey himself demonstrated a fluent grasp of its essentials even before he visited Paris, and both must have become acquainted with the style principally through Banister. Humfrey's more thorough integration of French idioms, made after he had studied them at first hand, proves his perceptions to have been alive to subtle details that eluded Banister.

By the time Humfrey arrived in Paris, probably at the beginning of 1665, Lully's style had entered a significantly new phase. One facet of this was his attraction to church music where a freedom to concentrate on serious texts drew from him new dimensions of musical expression. As early as 1660 he had written a motet which one contemporary commentator described as 'admirablement

Banister

GB - Och 1183, f. 103^v

25

Ex. 7   Banister

GB - Och 1183, f. 111

harmonique'[14] (although the latter neglected to record its title),
and Lully's new levels of expression were achieved principally
through harmonic means. The new phase was confirmed in 1664
by his first, and perhaps finest *grand motet, Miserere mei Deus*.[15]
This was performed again in Holy Week 1666, and Humfrey may
well have heard it on that occasion as some of his finest music
strongly suggests its influence. Its grand design of a rich string
symphonie followed by verses of the psalm, set for a diversity of
combinations of soloists, chorus, and strings punctuated by related
string *ritournelles*, must have recalled to an Englishman the more
modest format of the Restoration verse anthem, and suggested
directions in which this could develop. Furthermore its penitential
text and the affecting means of expressing this musically would
have struck a particularly sympathetic response in Humfrey who
himself had a predilection for texts of this nature. *Miserere mei
Deus* is a milestone in Lully's output, and signals his mastery of the
expressive and structural skills that he had been progressively
developing over the previous decade. Lully now does make some

use of tonality as a structural element. The motet is constructed in five broad sections, each with a contrasting tonal centre, C minor, G minor, B flat major, G minor, and C minor, and these form a coherent mirror tonal design. The opening *symphonie* in C minor is 17 bars in length, and Lully now provides such a movement with a central modulation to the relative major at bar 9 (Ex. 8) marking an advance on his earlier practice. This new tonal control sacrificed none of his expressive harmonic fluidity which continued to characterize duple-time string movements such as the first sections of his *ouvertures*. Further structural unity is provided by the interval of a falling minor sixth which pervades melody and bass lines throughout the motet. In the first period of this *symphonie*, for example, it is found in the top part in bars 1–2 and 5, in the bass in bar 7, and the bass spans the same interval in bar 6. This example illustrates Lully's fondness, which almost amounts to a mannerism, for falling conjunct phrases, often of five notes, in the bass. There are instances in bars 2–4 and 4–5 of Ex. 8, in Exx. 5 and 9, and in many other places in the motet.

The vocal textures of the motet, whether solos, ensembles, or choruses, sustain the affecting mood by means of an emotive use of harmony and an angularity of melodic line, both of which had their origins in earlier Italian styles. The treble solo 'Ecce enim in iniquitatibus conceptus sum' (Ex. 9) takes as its starting point the fluid texture of the Italian arioso, but the sinuously chromatic melody in bars 2–3 is a refinement of Lully, and one that Humfrey was to use extensively and poignantly. It culminates in a concentrated integration between melody and bass lines in bar 13, and the pungent interval of a diminished seventh falling to the significant word 'mater' in bar 14. At the end of the treble solo 'Ne proiicias me' (Ex. 10), Lully breaks his final phrase with rests over the penultimate strong beat suggesting that the singer, broken by the weight of the emotion, is unable to sustain a continuous line. This powerful gesture had its origins in Italian practice, but was employed with greater assurance by Lully, and was appropriated to affecting ends by Humfrey. Lully's translation of these expressive idioms of solo vocal writing into ensemble textures, of which there are notable examples in this motet, provided Humfrey with a significant precedent for the design of the ensemble verses in the Restoration anthem.

Lully was the single most important foreign composer in Humfrey's formative experience. It was a strange accident of

Ex. 8

Lully

history that Humfrey came under his spell at precisely the time when Lully was solving musical problems that were most akin to those that would face Humfrey: the creation of a style of sacred music which could absorb the affecting and passionate language of contemporary dramatic music, and integrate into its design string movements that would contribute a compatible opulence and profundity.

The essence of the English Restoration style lies in the particular synthesis that each of its major composers made of recent

Italian and French styles together with the greater or lesser debt that each owed to his more distant English past. Such a synthesis was given a decisive impetus by the taste of Charles II, and was conditioned by the specific musical demands of the English court. Pelham Humfrey was more exclusively committed to the newer idioms than Locke, and more capable of mastering their technical subtleties and expressive potential than Cooke. Of all major composers of the Restoration, Humfrey was least indebted to his English past. He was not a natural contrapuntist, and unlike Locke, Blow and Purcell, he wrote no independent instrumental music, a medium in which each of those composers could demonstrate a fluent contrapuntal mastery. Humfrey's most subtle strengths lay in his response to words, their natural accentuations and their suggestive power, and in his emotive command of harmony. Both biases had characterized the finest English music since the beginning of the Renaissance, and they represent his most conspicuous debts to his English past. His particular vocabulary of harmony, however, owed less to older English practice, and more to recent Italian and French models than did the harmony of his major English contemporaries. Furthermore, unlike Locke and Blow whose advanced harmony is more inclined to result from a contrapuntal interaction of angular and disjunct lines, Humfrey's advanced harmony tends to be calculated in more intrinsically vertical terms. In his anthems, Humfrey evolved principles of structure that were equally an innovative amalgam of Italian and French practice. He regularly adopted the tonal unification both within and between sections that was beginning to characterize Italian composition, and by the mid-1660s was emerging, rather more modestly, in Lully. He could simultaneously unify a substantial piece through the recurrence of one or more motives, and he would have derived this method from Lully, and perhaps even from Locke. Humfrey's particular synthesis of Italian, French, and English styles made a decisive contribution to the consolidation of a distinctively English baroque idiom, and occasioned an output in which expressive texts were given affecting articulation by using some of the richest musical resources of the day.

III

THE ESSENCE OF HUMFREY'S STYLE

HUMFREY'S primary stimulus came from the expressions of a text, and significantly he wrote no music that was not associated with words. His response was customarily activated by a section of text with a uniformity of mood, and only rarely did he isolate specific words for an illustration that would deviate from the prevailing musical norm. Occasionally he set texts with overt dramatic contrasts in which he delineated opposing forces with a comparable contrast of musical resources, and such instances confirm his strengths as a musical dramatist. Perhaps the most striking of these is found within *By the waters of Babylon* (2.74–95) where the jeering Babylonians, characterized by the full chorus in rising homophony and triple time, are pitted against the lamenting Jews, characterized by a three-part verse in angular chromatic counterpoint and duple time (see Ex. 40).

Humfrey had a particular attraction to texts that expressed the affecting emotions, grief, penitence, supplication, and the tender, and these drew from him some of his finest work. He was also drawn to festive texts which occasioned some of his grandest work, but even these, such as *O give thanks unto the Lord*, could revert to more intimate expressions within them.

Like his greatest English predecessors, Humfrey was alive to the natural accentuations of words irrespective of any irregularity of tactus or phrase that might result. Indeed such irregularity could in Humfrey's hands become a powerful propulsive agent. In emotive arioso he often began an opening or significant word on a weak beat and prolonged it through the following strong beat thus suggesting a momentary reversal of the strong and weak pulses (2.19–20). Accentuation of a word could be achieved by anacrusial word underlay which also momentarily reversed strong and weak pulses. This technique had a long ancestry in English music and was common in Locke, Blow, and Purcell, but Humfrey used it only sparingly (17.118–19) which is symptomatic of his weaker links with his English past. In duple time, trochaic patterns beginning on a strong beat followed by a rest became a particular

way of reproducing the natural stress of a significant word. The opening of the third verse of *Lord teach us to number our days* (Ex. 11) begins with this trochaic pattern, and in its sequential repetition illustrates the idiom of beginning an important word on a weak beat discussed above. Such trochees originated in solo vocal lines, but Humfrey could use them equally effectively in ensembles (7.29, 9.67, 14.113). The reversal of this figure, creating an iambus or a 'scotch snap' ♩♪, is relatively common in Locke, Blow, and Purcell, but it is rare in Humfrey (see Ex. 52, and 6.49). A further means of stressing significant words was Humfrey's practice of breaking a melodic line with rests on successive strong beats (see Exx. 28 and 47). In his most affecting application of this idiom, he interrupted the voice with a rest on the penultimate strong beat immediately prior to the cadence (Ex. 12), (see also Exx. 18 and 52, and 38.13). Both forms of this gesture had their origins in Italian arioso, and in Lully (see Ex. 10), but Humfrey transferred them to more lyrical contexts and thus sharpened their impact.

Humfrey's vocal and harmonic practice owed their greatest debt to the style of Carissimi and his Italian contemporaries tempered by experiments in this style by earlier generations of Englishmen,

Ex. 12
49.32

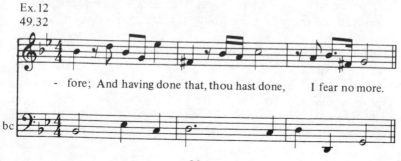

and by Italian elements in the practice of Lully. Although Humfrey's melody makes a calculated use of specifically expressive disjunct intervals, it is more generally conjunct than is that of Locke, Blow, and even much of Purcell's early work. Falling minor and diminished intervals had long had affective connotations in Italian music, and they became one of Humfrey's most affecting melodic devices. In his melody the interval in question customarily falls to a significant word on the major third of the chord, and it is preceded by an ascent of three or four conjunct notes which may be accompanied by contrary motion in the bass. Of the four species, falls of a diminished fourth (Ex. 13(i)), and a diminished fifth (see Ex. 15) are the most common in Humfrey. In the first case, the quitted note is usually dissonant, and in the second it is consonant. The fall of a minor sixth is not as common, and it is made from a dissonance (Ex. 13(ii)), (see also 9.16). The fall of the diminished seventh is the least common, and is made from a consonance (see Exx. 12 and 48, and also 14.91, 21.29, 22.48).

Ex. 13 (i)
12.56

Ex. 13 (ii)
13.100

b — Sheep of his pas-ture,

b — Lord in my trou-ble,

bc

Melodies built around arpeggio patterns were characteristic of both the extremes of declamatory recitative and the triple-time aria in Italian composers from the time of Carissimi, and became, less pervasively, one element of Humfrey's melodic style. He employed the arpeggio most boldly for declamation, such as at the opening of *Hear O heav'ns* (see Ex. 36), significantly his most Italianate anthem. Elsewhere the arpeggio could give a graphic realism to specific words or ideas (2.174, 13.155). In the festive anthems a text suggesting grandeur or praise could elicit an arpeggiated phrase (see Ex. 37(i), and also 15.127, 17.76, 18.31), and there are triple-time airs whose melody is built around arpeggios after the Italian manner (16.46 and 89). In the festive anthems short points of imitation built from an arpeggio are comparatively common (15.127, 17.104).

One of Humfrey's particularly distinctive melodic patterns is the sinuous chromatic line where sharp and flat inflexions of one note are juxtaposed in lines that trace and retrace their steps largely in conjunct movement. Some evidence of this practice can be found in Lully (see Ex. 9), but it was employed more pervasively by Humfrey who was quick to realize its concentrated harmonic properties. In his adult work, the inflexions usually progressively sharpen (see Ex. 30, and also 5.94, 9.38–41, 23.50–2, 45.32), but there are expressive instances of progressive flattening (see Exx. 33 and 48, and 7.19–20, 14.3). One phrase from *O Lord my God* illustrates both types (Ex. 14). In Humfrey, this idiom is found in either lightly-scored or homophonic textures where it becomes an agent of what is primarily a harmonic impulse.

The most powerful and particular aspect of Humfrey's expressive technique was his harmonic sensibility. Since the earliest stages of the *seconda prattica* the bass had played a decisive role in the propulsion of harmony, and so it remained in Humfrey's work.

Ex. 14
14.62

a   my heart al-so in the midst of my bo-dy, is ev'n like

bc

a   mel - ting wax,

bc

35

One of the simplest of Humfrey's bass patterns is the phrase of three conjunct notes descending a third, most commonly from the dominant to a first inversion of the tonic (10.24), and from the dominant in a minor key to the tonic of its relative major (5.56). This pattern is found in the music of the Italians, Lully (see Exx. 8 and 10), and Cooke, and pervades Humfrey's work where in many instances it is little more than a technical mannerism. In other cases, however, Humfrey turns it to a higher expressive end, and in the first verse of *By the waters of Babylon* it significantly contributes to the heavy lament of the exiles as it is extended sequentially and filters into the voice and obbligato lines (Ex. 15).

Ex. 15
2.22

The descending chromatic bass line was one of the most widespread means of expressing grief in Italian baroque music, and it was used with these connotations by Locke, Blow, and Purcell. It is, however, found only rarely in Humfrey's work, and then in contexts more structural than expressive. In a number of the anthems he used it to begin string movements, usually in triple time (2.131, 4a.1, 9.20, 10.64). As an expressive gesture it is seldom more than a few notes in length (see Ex. 34, and 7.41, 14.26), and thus far removed from the prototype. The only extended example is found in the Credo of the Service where at the words 'and was crucified' the bass descends by semitones through almost an octave (19.iv.31–4).

Another particular imprint is Humfrey's matching of a falling conjunct phrase in the bass with a rising conjunct phrase in the top part. This was found in Lully (see Ex. 8, bars 4–5) from whom he may have acquired it. Humfrey could employ it without apparent expressive intent (5.114), but more often he used it, like Lully, in a penitential context. The lines can be diatonic (5.94), but this imprint has a particular poignancy when one or both lines are chromatic (see Ex. 28, bar 133). Humfrey's most affecting application is his setting of 'and cast lots upon my vesture' in *O Lord my God* (Ex. 16) where the gradual separation of outer parts, and the chromatic inflexion in the alto create an augmented sixth chord.

Ex. 16
14.117

and cast   lots u-pon my   ves - ture.

Rising conjunct phrases in the bass are neither as common nor as potentially expressive as their falling counterparts. There are, none the less, examples at the beginnings of duple-time string movements (2.1, 13.1), and Humfrey may also have derived this usage from Lully (see Ex. 8). The only overtly illustrative example is found in the final chorus of *The King shall rejoice* where 'Be thou exalted Lord' (17.199) is set homophonically over a bass that rises through an octave.

A further idiomatic progression is the sequence in triple time propelled by a striding disjunct pattern in the bass. It customarily sets expressions of joy or praise, and in Humfrey's childhood anthem *Haste thee O God* the bass paced from one root position to another in a cycle predominantly of falling fifths (3.108). In his later work first inversions could replace some of the root positions, and the bass could rise a fourth and fall a third, but its essential striding propulsion remained (Ex. 17), (see also 5.197, 11.63, 11.101). In Ex. 17 the striding bass is mirrored by a disjunct,

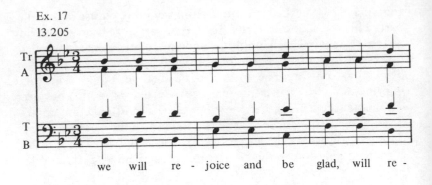

we will re - joice and be glad, will re -

- joice and be glad in it.

striding pattern in the top part. The antithesis of this idiom, which is no less particular to Humfrey, is the extension of a melodic phrase over a pedal. This is usually found in duple-time arioso where it implies ever more remote harmony, and heightens the tension of a penitential text (see Ex. 28, and 2.28). One of Humfrey's most moving examples occurs towards the climax of the first verse of *O Lord my God* (Ex. 18).

Considering the widespread incidence of thematic integration between outer parts in second generation composers of the *seconda prattica*, and in Locke and Blow, its virtual absence from Humfrey's vocal writing is surprising. The only example of any length accounts for the first five bars of the second verse of *Rejoice in the Lord O ye righteous* (16.46). Such integration as there is, is found most commonly at the outset of, or sometimes within duple-time sections of Humfrey's symphonies (9.1, 13.1, 14.37, 17.5).

One of the most pervasive of Humfrey's emphatic harmonic

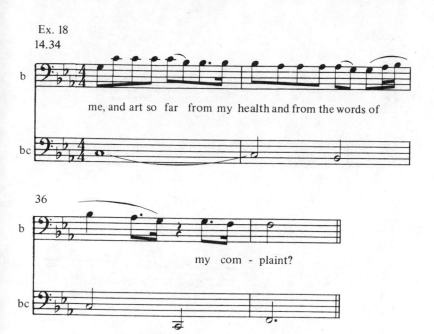

me, and art so far from my health and from the words of

36

my com - plaint?

gestures is the chord with a major third and a minor sixth. In the first verse of the childhood anthem *I will always give thanks*, he already demonstrated a confident handling of the chord where it stresses the most important word in the first phrase, 'thanks', and prevents any premature repose within that phrase (8.30). This chord can also contribute a heightened emphasis to the repetition of strategic words, particularly where one voice falls a diminished fourth from the minor sixth to the major third, outlining the upper constituents of the chord (see Ex. 47, bar 14, and 4b.28, 5.167, 17.112). The harmonic pungency of the chord can graphically set cries of despair as in an internal verse of *By the waters of Babylon*, and here the cries are reinforced by plaintive rising semitones (Ex. 19), (see also 7.6). This chord was not, however, exclusively associated with grief, and in the second, adult working of *Have mercy upon me O God* it paints the word 'joy' where it is immediately preceded by Humfrey's single use of the augmented fifth chord (Ex. 20). Although these two chords sound identical, their syntax and usage are wholly different.

Ex. 19

2.109

Ex. 20

4b.129

Another technique by which Humfrey heightened the expression of a word or an idea was by sharpening the sixth degree of the scale. This occasioned the augmented sixth chord which is found in Carissimi, and whose novelty in England after the Restoration was so admired by Dr Burney.[1] In solo textures only the extreme notes are present (5.133), but in vocal or instrumental ensembles inner parts could contribute a third (see Ex. 16), or an augmented fourth (23.214). There is in all Humfrey's work only one instance of the Neapolitan sixth progression, and that is in an instrumental symphony (2.135–6). Its expressive properties were not harnessed in English vocal music until the next generation.

In common with recent Italian practice, Humfrey treated the harmonic interval of the seventh with a freedom previously associated with the fifth. Its prominence in his only episode of five-part writing suggests that as he increased the number of parts, so he raised the composition of the triad to include the seventh (Ex. 21). Elsewhere points of imitation can enter on a seventh

Ex. 21
5.225 That I may dai - ly, may dai - ly per -

228 - form my vows.

(5.59, 10.40), and one short ritornello actually begins with a chord of the seventh (17.78). The seventh appears to have had connotations of vehemence for Humfrey, and he employed it at the culmination of the Babylonians' taunts in *By the waters of Babylon* (see Ex. 40), and to set 'power' at the climax of a phrase in *When from his throne* (23.258). In Italian baroque music, consecutive sevenths and their inversion consecutive seconds had long served to sustain harmonic and emotional tension at the highest level right up to the repose of the cadence (see Ex. 1). Both forms were appropriated by Humfrey with a confident realization of their expressive potential. Such consecutives are found between two upper parts (see Exx. 19 and 27, and also 14.160, 20.4), and between the outer parts (see Ex. 28, and also 11.59, 13.12) where they need not precede a final cadence.

There are occasional examples of the chord of the dominant minor ninth in Humfrey's work, but its treatment has none of the freedom that he allowed the seventh. He used it illustratively to suggest pathos (see Ex. 15), the turbulence of the elements (6.123), and a jubilant mood (12.35, 15.108). More extensive use of chords of the ninth on other degrees of the scale did not emerge until Purcell's work.

Humfrey's harmony is permeated with the juxtaposition of diatonic notes and their chromatic alteration either in the same part, involving the sinuously chromatic melodic line already described, or between different parts involving the more traditional cross relation. One of his most distinctive phrases of chromatic alteration is found in two progressions each of three chords in which the bass moves from the subdominant to the dominant. In the more common variety (Ex. 22) a flattened third over the subdominant is sharpened, after which the bass moves to the dominant with a major third above. Both the second and third chords of this progression usually include a seventh in another part. This progression is usually found at a cadence, but it can occur within a phrase (4b.39). In the second variety of the progression (Ex. 23) a major third over the subdominant is raised to a perfect fourth after which the bass moves to the dominant with a major third above. There is usually a seventh in another part in the second chord of this progression, and in this example from the third symphony of *O Lord my God*, the cross relation in the viola adds an additional piquancy.

There are three species of cross relation which are particularly symptomatic of Humfrey's harmonic sensitivity, and contribute to the individuality of his harmonic palette. The first involves two parts falling an interval of a third in parallel thirds where the first note of the lower part is raised a semitone by the second note of the upper part.[2] This is found between the upper parts of string textures (13.112–13, 18.21–2), between the outer parts of string

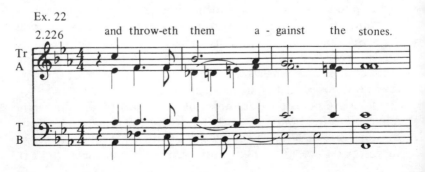

Ex. 22

2.226　　and throw-eth them　　a - gainst　the　stones.

textures (see Ex. 23), and in vocal textures it can directly intensify the pathos of the text (Ex. 24). Such a cross relation can produce the first of the two types of sharpening over a subdominant root discussed in the previous paragraph (7.54, 18.80). The second species of cross relation common in Humfrey is occasioned by one part falling to the sharpened inflexion of a note whose flattened form is simultaneously sounding in another part (Ex. 25), (see also 10.3, 14.8, 15.135, 18.60). The third cross relation is a single

Ex. 23
14.137

Ex. 24
10.47   dai - ly say   un - to   me,

Ex. 25
16.79   sing   to the   Lord

instance where the sharpened sixth and seventh degrees of a minor scale rising towards the tonic are uncompromisingly pitted against the same degrees flattened as they fall from the tonic (Ex. 26). This phrase includes at bar 39 another example of the cross relation between two outer parts moving in parallel thirds.

Ex. 26

In most of these cases of chromatic inflexion, the note of the chord affected is the third. Cross relations involving the third had long been a distinctive characteristic of English harmonic practice, but whereas formerly they had tended to cluster over dominant-like degrees, in Humfrey they are more inclined to involve the subdominant. Significantly, Humfrey never used the so-called 'English cadence' figure involving a cross relation between major and minor third over the dominant. This figure was nevertheless a distinctive feature of the music of Locke, Blow, and Purcell, and Humfrey's avoidance of it again reflects his weaker links with his English past.

Among major composers of the Restoration, Humfrey inclined least naturally towards prolonged counterpoint. His contrapuntal lines are invariably anchored to a strong harmonic foundation from which they grow (2.60, 10.151). There is no suggestion that his harmony is determined for any length of time by a contrapuntal interaction of angular lines such as is common in Locke, Blow, and Purcell. Humfrey's most regular and sustained imitative counterpoint lies in his two- and three-part ensemble verses. Here points of imitation tend to be comparatively long, although the answering voice is inclined to enter before the point is completed (2.187, 14.52). Humfrey could adopt a declamatory or parlando phrase as a point (see Ex. 14, and also 4b.115), as had been

44

common in small-scale Italian sacred vocal polyphony around the 1620s, and in each case the starkness of the point was designed to capture the mood of the text. Yet another common type of point was that built around arpeggio patterns (15.127, 17.104). Elsewhere points could be terse and only partially imitated (2.60). An idiomatic contrapuntal texture that Humfrey evolved to meet a particular expressive need is found where one voice imitates another at a single beat's distance. The resultant sense of displacement of vertical alignment, a loss of synchronization, can vividly illustrate expressions of dislocation in a text (Ex. 27), (see also 2.111–16). Each of these examples culminates in consecutive sevenths or seconds prior to the cadence.

Humfrey's four-part counterpoint is seldom extensive, and is often introduced into his longer choruses to lend some textural contrast. After the exposition of a point in such instances, he either introduced another point (10.151), or resumed homophonic writing (4b.148). His most prolonged four-part imitative episode is

Ex. 27

45

found in the final chorus of *By the waters of Babylon* (2.203–29), but even this is punctuated by homophonic phrases. Other contrapuntal textures in two to four parts can vary from the sporadically imitative to those where the voices merely maintain some expressive independence of line.

The most important single formative influence on Humfrey's vocal and harmonic language was provided by the Italian style which he experienced either directly, or through the music of Lully and Locke. The formal mediums and structures in which Humfrey organized his vocal language also owed a major debt to Italian practice. The styles of his vocal writing tend to be distinguished, after the Italian manner, by his choice of time signature where duple time serves declamatory and arioso episodes, and triple time serves more lyrical episodes. Humfrey had recourse to dry recitative only rarely, and then specifically for bold declamation (see Ex. 36), or to paint a bleak text (14.102). Solo textures in duple time lyrical enough to be classified as airs are also uncommon. They are found principally among the secular songs where they set metrical texts, and fall into the robust style of the duple-time ballad which began to supplant the more emotive arioso in this medium from about 1670. A rare example in the anthems is the treble verse 'From the ends of the earth' in *Hear my crying O God* (5.85).

The majority of Humfrey's writing for solo voice in duple time can be classified as some species of arioso characterized by deft word setting, and an irregularity of phrase length and harmonic rhythm, all designed to enliven the emotional subtleties and fluctuations of the text. A bass verse in *Like as the hart* (Ex. 28) demonstrates the dramatic skill with which Humfrey welded the constituents of his language into a concentrated and cumulative expression of grief. The mood of urgency is set from the start by the bass voice declaiming 'why' on a weak beat and immediately interrupting his first phrase with a rest. At the height of that phrase, which has to this point moved conjunctly, the voice falls a diminished fifth to the third of the chord setting the significant word 'full', and in bar 130 the word 'O' is emphasized by anacrusial underlay. The repetition of the last three words in bar 131 is given a particular impact by beginning on a strong beat, by an absence of anacrusial underlay, and by the chromatic bass note in the continuo. The repetition of the whole text from bar 132 places the voice in a higher and thus more insistent register, and

46

Ex. 28

the harmonic rhythm accelerates. The cries 'why' on two successive weak beats following rests on the preceding strong beats in bar
132, lend a pungent realism to these interrogatory exclamations.
Its consequent phrase gathers momentum as voice and continuo
lines separate largely by conjunct movement culminating at bar
134 in consecutive sevenths. From the end of bar 134 two
sequential statements of the text, the second an insistent third
higher than the first, are built over a pedal. By bar 137 Humfrey
has stated his complete text, and this inner structural point is
marked by a modulation to A flat, the relative major of the key in
which the verse began. From here he makes emphatic repetition of
key phrases of text, and the voice gradually rises in tessitura. In
bars 138 and 139, still on successive weak beats, 'why' is given an
added vehemence by twice creating unprepared sevenths with the
continuo. In bar 140 'O' is expanded with a rising semitone
melisma accompanied by falling conjunct movement in the continuo. The verse culminates in bar 142 with 'why' sung twice on
successive strong beats separated by a rest, which gives these final
statements a conclusive impact. This solo verse is the first part of a
broader binary structure. It ends on the dominant of F minor, and
the tonic is restored by the following ensemble verse.

Humfrey's most extended lyrical writing for solo voice is found
in his triple-time airs where melody becomes the principal element, and breadth and symmetry its primary components. Their
texts have none of the emotive content of those he set as arioso,
and they were more simply set. Whole sentences or phrases could
be repeated, but momentary intensifications are foreign to this
style. The harmonic pulse tends to be more regular than in the
arioso, and the rhythm can reflect the influence of dance patterns.
The first verse of *O praise the Lord* (Ex. 29) is one of Humfrey's
most accomplished triple-time airs. Each half of its binary structure makes an unadorned statement of the same verse of the text,
and each half is symmetrically balanced with an identical and
cumulative phrase structure of $2 + 3 + 4$ bars. The air is not static,
however, and in each half the harmonic rhythm accelerates in
successive phrases. The tessitura of the air progressively rises and
culminates in the first phrase of the second half at bar 46 which is
an inversion of the opening of the verse. The rhythm of the verse is
dominated by ♩♩.♪ and its extensions which originated probably
in the contemporary French sarabande (see Ex. 5). Dramatic
writing in triple time is rare in Humfrey's music (6.47), and the

single extensive example, in *The Masque of the Three Devils* in *The Tempest* is remarkable in that it abandons the Italian dramatic conventions of duple and triple time and adopts the French style of hybrid declamation and lyricism in triple time (see Ex. 50).

The bipartite vocal structure evolved by second generation composers of the Italian *seconda prattica* (see Ex. 2) had already appeared on a modest scale in England prior to the Restoration in masque and theatre music. Humfrey made only limited use of it in solo vocal writing in the anthems (10.94, 12.49), but used it extensively in his songs (24, 29, 30, 32, 48, 52). He expanded the bipartite structure in the odes to include at least three sections, each with a contrasting time-signature, and some of the latter include the faster dance measures ⊅ and 6i that were not used in the anthems (see Exx. 42 and 43). In the anthems the bipartite structure is more common in ensemble verses (2.103, 13.115), and the change from duple to triple time often became a significant structural point where a new key centre could be defined, or additional voices could be introduced (11.89).

One particularly idiomatic type of ensemble verse in Humfrey's work is what might be called the subject-answer dialogue. In its basic form, one voice announces its minor-key subject which comes to a half close on the dominant. This is answered by a second solo voice with a phrase that can bear only a slight resemblance to the subject, but which becomes its consequent moving to a full close in the relative major. At this point one or two further solo voices can continue the solo dialogue, and when all have entered, they join a concerted ensemble with some derivation of the subject usually in its original tonic (see Ex. 34, and also 11.41, 17.34).

Another particular species of ensemble in Humfrey is the dialogue in which three or four voices exchange phrases either as soloists or in partial ensemble (4b.131, 14.111). Such dialogues could serve a dramatic purpose, and probably originated in the dramatic dialogues of earlier Italian vocal music and pre-Restoration English masque music. Humfrey's most effective, and overtly dramatic dialogues make up much of *Hear O heav'ns* as the opening of its second half confirms (Ex. 30).

A number of Humfrey's solo verses in duple time introduce a solo violin obbligato (see Ex. 15, and also 5.85, 13.157). Such obbligatos were found in Carissimi, Lully, and Locke, although Humfrey's obbligatos are never as extensive as Locke's. The

49

Ex. 29

15.37

O praise the Lord, laud ye the name of the Lord, praise it O ye ser - vants of the Lord, O praise the Lord, laud ye the

name of the Lord, praise it O ye

ser - vants of the Lord.

addition of one or more upper strings to accompany a solo voice growing out of Locke's practice was explored further in the music of Blow and Purcell.

In Humfrey's music, there is as much variety in the types of solo voices used as in the textures they created. He showed a preference for the tenor, assigning to it the majority of his lyrical solos, and making it the only voice to divide in ensembles. This preference may reflect the fact that Humfrey himself sang tenor. During the Restoration there were two distinct types, the upper tenor whose range was d to g', and the lower or tenor-bass whose range was A to e' flat (5.124, 13.99). The solo bass had the widest range spanning F to e' flat, and Humfrey assigned it both his most dramatic solo writing, including the role of Neptune in *The Masque of Neptune* in Act V of *The Tempest* (2.168, 13.155, 14.102, 51.13 ff), and more lyrical episodes of arioso (see Ex. 11). The tessitura of his chorus bass is uniformly about a minor third lower. He seldom gave the solo alto any particular prominence in his church music (4b.94) which is surprising given the excellence of William Turner, his childhood collaborator and fellow Gentlemen of the Chapel, and the elaborate writing for solo alto that followed in the work of Blow and Purcell. There is no suggestion yet of the

7.34

distinction between high and low alto that is found in Purcell's later work. Humfrey's most extensive alto solos are found in the odes and the tripartite song for Aeolus in *The Masque of Neptune* in *The Tempest* (51.69–97), and these would almost certainly have been written for Turner. In Humfrey's lifetime the solo treble voice diminished in both prominence and range. The bulk of his writing for solo treble is found in the childhood verse anthems (6.47 and 85), and treble solos in the adult anthems are rare (5.85).

The treble's most usual range was about e′ to f″ with an occasional c′ and g″.

The mainspring of Humfrey's art lies in his writing for solo voices either alone or in ensemble, and in the anthems, odes, and theatre music, the chorus fulfils only a minor role. In the odes, the chorus acts as a refrain repeating the text and usually musical material from the previous verse. There are customarily at least two choruses in the anthems, and the more substantial one concludes the anthem. This chorus can adopt a bipartite structure in which the duple section can be homophonic and the triple imitative (17.199, 18.172). The final chorus was often completed with three or four homophonic bars in duple time, a custom that had its origins in earlier Italian practice (12.122, 13.264, 17.252, 18.195). In some anthems the final chorus is merely a repetition of the central chorus (14, 15). Elsewhere the central chorus can act as a refrain repeating the words and usually musical material from the previous verse (10.56, 11.101, 12.75).

If Humfrey's vocal music owed its principal formative debt to the Italian style, the techniques of his string writing owe their principal debt to French models. All but two of the anthems, and all the odes, have string movements, and in all but one of the adult anthems, the writing is in four parts. The symphony, the most substantial of Humfrey's string movements, is derived from the earlier type of Lully's French *ouverture* (see Ex. 5), and customarily falls into two sections. The first in duple time is characterized by a stately solemnity, a predominance of dotted rhythms, irregular phrase lengths and fluctuating harmony all of which prevent any sense of internal repose. A half close in the tonic provides the only real point of internal punctuation. Humfrey's second section is triple in time, binary in structure, homophonic in texture, and characterized by some form of the French sarabande rhythm ♩♩·♪|♩·♪♩. Phrase lengths tend to be short and regular. This section is invariably in the tonic established by the first section, and either comes to a half close or modulates to a related key at the internal double bar. In Humfrey's simpler triple-time sections, the bass provides only a slow–moving foundation (6.1–30), but more usually it contributes a vigorous integrated involvement (11.19–24, 12.1–9). The last four bars of the triple-time section are almost invariably repeated softly.

The opening symphonies of the majority of anthems and of all the odes contain both sections, and either the whole symphony or just its triple section is usually repeated at the centre of the work. Only in *O be joyful* does the opening symphony bear any thematic relation to the verse that follows, and the particular reason for this will be examined in Chapter IV. In some anthems the opening symphony consists of the triple section alone (6, 12, 18), and in the three finest penitential anthems it consists of only the duple section (2, 10, 14). Each of the latter has a substantial triple-time movement entitled symphony at its centre compensating for its omission earlier.

Only in two anthems is the symphony the sole instrumental movement (6, 12). In the majority, vocal episodes are punctuated by ritornellos which derive their function and substance from Italian and French prototypes. In their simplest form, and adhering most closely to their models, they simply echo vocal material (5.144, 11.67). More usually, however, Humfrey's ritornellos take a phrase from a verse and extensively develop it (5.184, 13.140). A further type of ritornello, only remotely related to vocal material, is a substantial movement which assumes the proportions and stylistic characteristics of the symphony (13.109, 17.219). Less common types of ritornello can provide short complementary interjections (17.78), a short modulating episode (10.124), or a recurrent structural buttress (13.52, 18.58).

Although Humfrey's string movements took French models as their starting point, they differ from their prototypes in their harmonic richness, and in the distinctive activity of their inner parts. Lully is reputed to have left the composition of inner parts in his dramatic music to his *secrétaires* Lallouette and Collasse, but even in the opening *symphonie* of *Miserere mei Deus* (see Ex. 8), the three inner parts create no more than passing diatonic dissonance. Humfrey's inner parts often make a definitive contribution to the harmonic and rhythmic character of their movements. This is most apparent in the odes where there are ritornellos (and choruses) which add two inner parts to an otherwise exact repetition of the preceding solo verse (22.113, 23.90, 23.147). Such harmonic and rhythmic vigour gave Humfrey's instrumental movements a character and propulsion that distinguished them from their models, and were to leave their mark on English string writing until the end of the century.

In the anthem, his most elaborate form, Humfrey took as his model the multi-sectional structure that had been evolved by Cooke and employed by Locke, but he went on to expand its design while reducing the number of its constituent divisions. He achieved this by imposing on the whole anthem and on its internal sections a rigorous tonal order such as was beginning to characterize Italian composition. Each section is usually in the tonic of the anthem, and is given an internal binary structure which permits a more controlled and extensive thematic expansion than is found in the anthems of Cooke. All but two of the anthems (13, 16) are in minor keys, and each section thus proceeds towards an internal point of modulation in the relative major. Such points assume a wider structural significance, and can additionally signal a change of metre or texture. In some of his more extensive anthems, Humfrey experimented with longer internal paragraphs each made up of a number of sections, and one or two of these sections within the paragraph could be wholly in a related key. Thus he evolved broader ternary tonal structures such as he would have encountered in Lully's *Miserere mei Deus*.

Humfrey created further structural coherence in his more extensive anthems by means of short, recurrent thematic motives. These were customarily of four or five notes, and he probably also recognized this species of unification in the work of Lully. Humfrey's application of tonal and motivic unification will be examined more closely in the next chapter where individual works will be considered in their entirety.

Simpler coherence was achieved by the wholesale repetition of a section or sections at a subsequent point or points in the anthem or ode. The most common examples are repetition of the symphony or part of it at the centre, and repetition of the central chorus at the end. Elsewhere a ritornello could recur (13, 18), or the first group of sections could be repeated towards the end of the anthem (9, 12, 13, 15, 18). The most complex example of such unification is the quasi-rondo structure of *Rejoice in the Lord O ye righteous*.

Although Humfrey's style was definitively shaped by his particular synthesis of Italian and French practice, that synthesis was made by a musician with a recognizable English identity. His style found its most powerful expression in the English verse anthem revitalizing it with an emotional content and technical resource which restored the anthem to a peak of refinement it had not enjoyed for about half a century. Furthermore this artistic restoration provided the basis for the expansions and diversifications of the medium by Blow and Purcell in the ensuing decades.

IV

THE CHURCH MUSIC

Two of Humfrey's anthems, the first working of *Have mercy upon me O God*, and *Haste thee O God*, together with his contribution to the 'Club' anthem, *I will always give thanks*, its symphony, first two verses, and central chorus (8.1–89), are known to date from his boyhood. The texts of four childhood verse anthems additional to *Haste thee O God* were printed in James Clifford's *The Divine Services and Anthems* (1664), but their music has not survived. These are *The heavens declare the glory of God*, *It is a good thing to give thanks*, *Bow down thine ear*, and *The Lord declared his salvation*, the last of which was composed for the King's birthday on 29 May. On stylistic grounds, *Almighty God who mad'st thy blessed son*[1] and *Hear my prayer O God* can almost certainly be added to the boyhood anthems. All five extant works reflect the dominant influence of Cooke in format, textures, and to some extent in language, yet they also suggest the wider horizons that Humfrey found in Locke and Banister. Behind their eclecticism, however, a recognizable musical individuality is clearly beginning to emerge.

Each of the five extant boyhood anthems begins with a string movement independent of any vocal material, and except for the lame overture of *Have mercy upon me O God* I, these represent Humfrey's earliest essays in the French style. The symphonies of *Almighty God* and *Haste thee O God* contain both duple and triple sections, although in the former they are separated by the first verse; those of *Hear my prayer O God* and the 'Club' anthem contain only the triple section. Neither section in any of the symphonies has yet achieved a complete stylistic consistency. In the duple section of *Haste thee O God*, phrases of dotted quavers can yield to even quavers, although in *Almighty God* the dotted idiom predominates. In the triple sections, the French sarabande rhythm ♩♩.♪ | ♩.♪♩ can be seen gradually emerging from one or other bars of the pattern, although the complete pattern almost dominates the first half of the triple section of *Hear my prayer O God* and the second half of that in *Almighty God* (1.45). Of the childhood anthems, only *Have mercy upon me O God* I has any

56

internal ritornellos, and these all echo immediately preceding vocal material in the manner of Cooke.

Humfrey's four complete childhood anthems are all distinguished by a prominence given to the treble and bass voices in verses, and by the high f"s and g"s demanded of the treble voice in both verses and choruses. These characteristics are demonstrably derived from the practice of Cooke, and do not recur in Humfrey's adult work. In both *Almighty God* and *Have mercy upon me O God* I there are substantial verses for two trebles and a bass (1.53, 4a.111), and in *Hear my prayer O God* the majority of verses are for either treble or bass, or for both together.

Some of the childhood anthems further reflect the style of Cooke in their prominent instances of notated embellishments of the type that Cooke is known to have improvised (6.49, 6.55, 6.72). One example from *Have mercy upon me O God* I (Ex. 31) illustrates how such embellishment could arrest the harmony, and suggests one reason why such embellishment is absent from Humfrey's later work. Other symptoms of the stage before Humfrey's style had settled into the homogeneity of his maturity include the change of key-signature in *Have mercy upon me O God* I (4a.100), the change of time-signature in mid-phrase in *Hear my prayer O God* (6.122), and the two-bar interjection of the chorus in the manner of Cooke in *Haste thee O God* (3.131). Two of the childhood anthems contain Humfrey's only use in the church music of an Italianate melodic mannerism where an anticipatory dissonance resolves by unexpectedly leaping up a third (Ex. 32), (see also Ex. 35). This mannerism was common in Locke, and is found in Blow and Purcell, but did not recur in Humfrey's adult church music.

With the exception of the shorter *Almighty God*, the complete childhood anthems are all about the same length as the anthems of

Ex. 31
4a.52

that thou might'st be justi-fied, be jus - - ti - fied

Ex. 32

1.67

car - nal lusts,

Cooke, yet they contain fewer internal divisions. Some of their constituent sections contain Humfrey's first attempts at imposing an ordered tonal design which, even as early as this, he seems to have recognized would allow a more carefully calculated expansion of his thematic material. The lack of a consistent tonal organization throughout the very early *Have mercy upon me O God* I causes it to wander arbitrarily, and contributes to its conspicuous inferiority.

Haste thee O God and his contribution to the 'Club' anthem bring Humfrey to the threshold of a maturity of style and technique which was realized fully after his three years abroad. The progress towards that maturity is most clearly illustrated by a comparison of the childhood version of *Have mercy upon me O God* with Humfrey's substantial reworking of it as an adult, and a comparative analysis of the two is found in Fig. 3. In his revision he first discarded its lame overture and three ritornellos, thus omitting strings altogether, and replaced the original repetitious 'Halleluia' with an additional verse from the psalm to provide the final chorus. Although it is ten bars longer than the first working, the second working has only seven internal sections compared to the former eleven. Each section of the second has a calculated tonal design, and the final verse is made up of three sections expanded into a ternary tonal plan which proceeds from C minor to G major and returns to C minor. These designs facilitated a development of thematic material which was not found in the earlier working. The first verse of the latter, for example, had a number of internal modulations each separated by only four or five bars, and these fragmented rather than expanded the section. The move to C major for the final sections in the first working is the only instance in an anthem where Humfrey changed the mode within a work, and significantly he rejected this in the second.

	First Working				Second Working			
	scoring	bars	t-s	key	scoring	bars	t-s	key
Overture	a3	19	4/4	C min	—	—	—	—
Have mercy upon me	atb	17	4/4	C min	atb	24	4/4	C min
Ritornello	continuo	5	4/4	C min	—	—	—	—
Wash me throughly	t ⎡	17	4/4	C min to B flat	b	20	4/4	E flat to C min
For I acknowledge	⎣				TrATB	5	4/4	E flat to C min
Against thee only	a2	5		B flat	t	44	3/4	C min
Ritornello	atb ⎡	37	4/4	G min to C min	—	—	—	—
Behold I was shapen					a ⎡	18	4/4	C min
But lo thou requirest	⎣				⎣			
Thou shalt purge me	atb	8	3/4	C maj	tb	9	4/4	C min to G
Thou shalt make me	a3	3	4/4	C maj	atb ⎡	10	3/4	G to G maj
Ritornello	trb	8	3/4	C maj	⎣	—	—	—
That the bones	—	—	—	—	atb	10	4/4	G maj to C min
Turn thou thy face	trtrb	12	3/4	C maj	TrATB	15	4/4	C min
Halleluia	TrATB	12	3/4	C maj	—	—	—	—
		2	4/4	C maj				

4a total length: 145 bars 4b total length: 155 bars

FIGURE 3 Comparative Analyses of the two workings of *Have mercy upon me O God*

The only musical material to be substantially reworked in the second version is that of the first verse, and the opening of each will illustrate how Humfrey's technique and expressive capacities became more polished between his childhood and adult years (Exx. 33 and 34). Both begin with versions of the subject–answer dialogue, but in the first its organization was not yet fully determined, and the third voice entered only with the ensemble. Much of the refinement of the second working begins with its word setting. In the earlier working the tenor began on the first beat of the bar, and his first four words were set within the range of a minor third. In the later, the tenor begins more effectively on a weak beat, and his first four words are set within the wider range of a minor sixth allowing a more expressive melodic contour, and a more prominent accentuation of important words. Furthermore, in the second working Humfrey repeats smaller verbal phrases thus permitting a greater flexibility of phrase length, emphasis on significant words, and a smoother propulsion of the texture. The new point after the half close on the dominant is retained in the later working, but it now begins on the fifth rather than the third of the chord, is enlivened rhythmically, and contains repetition of one of its verbal phrases all of which realize an altogether more fluent continuity.

Humfrey's only other adult anthem without strings is *Hear O heav'ns*, but in more striking ways it remains the most atypical. Totalling only 72 bars, it is his shortest anthem, it is wholly in duple time, and it consists of only four sections, two substantial dialogue verses for atb and two shorter choruses, all of which are thematically linked. *Hear O heav'ns* is also Humfrey's most overtly Italianate anthem, and it is strikingly similar to the style of the three-part declamatory motet by Carissimi represented by *Turbabuntur impii*. This particular motet, originally the opening of the oratorio *Damnatorum lamentatio*, dates from 1666, and Humfrey may have heard it during his travels. In any case it is found in a near-contemporary English manuscript source,[2] and was thus known in Restoration England. A comparison of its opening (Ex. 35) with that of *Hear O heav'ns* (Ex. 36) points to the stylistic origins of Humfrey's anthem. Both begin with a declamatory phrase built around an arpeggio, and supported by almost static harmony which accelerates only towards the cadence. Each of Humfrey's verses remains firmly anchored to C minor, and each chorus begins in E flat and returns to C minor. Primary structural

Ex. 33

Ex. 34

coherence is provided not by tonality, but by the recurrence of the ascending motive G, A, B flat, B natural, C, or by its first three notes, and both of these pervade the anthem.

Of all Humfrey's anthems, the one closest to the style and proportions of Lully's *grand motet*, in terms of its substantial length, the relative importance of its string movements and chorus, the prominent verse–chorus antiphony, and its wide-ranging tonal structures, is *O give thanks unto the Lord*. Further-more the quality of its invention, its sustained and concentrated development, and its richly varied resources combine to make it

Ex. 36

7.1

also Humfrey's most magnificent anthem. Its text and scale suggest that it may have been written for Easter Day or some other special celebration in the Chapel Royal. Rather than being built from a succession of sections all in the tonic, it consists of three broader paragraphs, each with a number of internal sections (Fig. 4). The outer paragraphs, sections 1 and 2, and 8 to 10, have a tonal centre of B flat, while the central paragraph, sections 3 to 7, has a tonal centre of D minor which gives the anthem, like Lully's

		scoring	bars	t-s	key	
1i	Symphony	a4	12	4/4	B flat	
ii			24	3/4	B flat	
2i	O give thanks	TrATB	16	3/4	B flat to F	
ii	Ritornello	a4	13	3/4	F to B flat	develops 2i
iii		TrATB	21	3/4	B flat	extends 2i
iv	Ritornello	a4	12	3/4	B flat	repeats 2ii
3	I called	tt	10	4/4	B flat to D min	
4	Ritornello	a4	7	4/4	D min	
5i	I will thank	at	7	4/4	D min to A	
ii			18	3/4	A to D min	
6	Ritornello	a4	14	3/4	D min	develops 5ii
7i	The same stone	b, vn	5	4/4	D min to A	
ii			15	3/4	A to G min	
8i	Ritornello	a4	4	3/4	G min	anticipates 8ii
ii	This is the day	TrATB & attb	16	3/4	G min to D	based on 2i
iii	Ritornello	a4	3	3/4	B flat	develops 8ii
iv		TrATB & attb	12	3/4	B flat	develops 8ii
v	Ritornello	a4	6	3/4	B flat	develops 8ii
vi	Help me now	attb	4	4/4	B flat to G min	
vii			8	3/4	G min to B flat	
viii	Ritornello	a4	4	3/4	B flat	
ix	Thou art	TrATB & attb	20	3/4	B flat	develops 8ii
x	Ritornello	a4	12	3/4	B flat	develops 8ix
9	O give thanks					repeats 2i, 2ii, and 2iii
10	His mercy	TrATB	4	4/4		

Total length (excluding 9): 267 bars

FIGURE 4   A Sectional Analysis of Humfrey's anthem *O give thanks unto the Lord*

Miserere mei Deus, an overall ternary structure. Furthermore sections 2 and 8 are built on a single pervasive thematic idea which permeates all subsections, and lends its own species of binding unity. The prolonged episodes of antiphony between attb ensemble verse and the chorus that characterize section 8 of *O give thanks unto the Lord* are demonstrably indebted to the antiphony between *petit choeur* and *grand choeur* in Lully's motet.

The only other anthem by Humfrey in a major key is *Rejoice in the Lord O ye righteous* which is one of the finest of his smaller festive works. It is also uncharacteristic in being almost wholly in triple time, and in being the only anthem with string ritornellos to lack a symphony. Although most of its sections are in B flat with prominent internal modulation, at the centre of the anthem (16.70–108) there is a longer paragraph, consisting of two verses separated by a ritornello, which moves to an inner tonal centre of F minor/major and introduces a richness of chromatic harmony more usual in the penitential anthems. Humfrey repeats the first verse and ritornello twice, giving the anthem an overall rondo structure ABACAD where C is the longer internal paragraph and D is the single chorus at the end. Further coherence is provided by the arpeggio patterns which pervade each of the verses.

From its many near-contemporary sources, *O praise the Lord* appears to have been one of Humfrey's most popular anthems during the Restoration period. Apart from its opening tenor air discussed in Chapter III, all its verses are ensembles. These are imposing rather than expressive, and the relentlessly festive mood denies this work the affecting contrasts of *O give thanks unto the Lord*. Despite its length, *O praise the Lord* contains no internal paragraphs with tonal contrast.

The King shall rejoice sets a text closely associated with royal celebrations, and a note at the head of an early copy in the Sibley manuscript at the Eastman School of Music, Rochester, states that it was composed for the birthday of Charles II on 29 May,[3] although it makes no mention of the year. Two days before his diary ceases, Pepys mentioned 'a good anthem of Pelham's' on the King's birthday in 1669 and this may have been the year, although it is not unlikely that Humfrey would have provided the anthem for this occasion in subsequent years, as he had provided *The Lord declared his salvation* for the King's birthday during his boyhood. *The King shall rejoice* is among Humfrey's longest and grandest anthems with ten string movements, and the majority of its verses scored for attb. Despite its 254 bars, there are only seven principal sections, within which there is extensive development of material. None of these, however, deviates from the tonal centre of D minor.

Although it too sets a festive text, *Thou art my king O God* is not cast on as grand a scale as *The King shall rejoice*. Word setting is more finely calculated than in some of the other festive works, and much of its invention is intrinsically more expressive. Each of its sections is in C minor, and the anthem's coherence relies on a repetition of the symphony at the centre and, in common with other festive anthems, a repetition of the first verse and ritornello towards the end. Its single ritornello appears at no fewer than four significant points thus providing the anthem additionally with a series of internal structural buttresses. Further unity is provided by a thematic affinity between the openings of the first two verses (18.31 and 70).

Lift up your heads is the least accomplished of Humfrey's adult anthems, and contains suggestions of hasty and uncritical composition. These include the sudden deceleration of harmonic rhythm from bar 4 of its symphony, and the short phrases and frequent cadences in many of the vocal sections. Furthermore the repetition after bar 91 of the whole anthem, excluding the duple section of the symphony, with a final extension of only 19 bars to complete the work, betrays both haste and perhaps a loss of interest in material which may have proved comparatively intractable. All is not inferior, however, and the short dramatic exchanges between solo alto and tenor asking 'who is the king of glory?' and the chorus's confident response (9.80–91) are of an altogether higher calibre.

The last of the festive anthems, *O be joyful*, is unique in Humfrey's output in that each half of its triple-time symphony develops a phrase drawn respectively from the beginning (see Ex. 37(i)) and the centre (see Ex. 37(ii)) of its first verse. The symphony of Locke's *O be joyful* also anticipated its first verse (see Fig. 2), and as such anticipations were common in Locke, this single instance in Humfrey suggests that the younger man may have been influenced by Locke's setting of the same text which he had known since boyhood. Further comparison of the two settings discloses additional affinities. Three phrases from Humfrey's anthem (Ex. 37) are thematically similar to Locke's settings of the same words (Ex. 38). As the first two phrases by Humfrey and the first by Locke serve as the basis of their respective symphonies, the affinities between the two anthems become all the more sustained. Hereafter, however, the differences become even more significant. Although Humfrey's anthem seems at first glance only four bars longer than Locke's, lacking a counterpart of Locke's 26-bar Gloria, it is in reality considerably more extensive. A comparison of its sectional analysis (Fig. 5) with that of Locke's anthem (see Fig. 2) shows it to have fewer internal sections, and almost all of

Ex. 37 (i)   Humfrey

O be joy - ful in the Lord all ye lands,

serve the Lord with glad - ness,

For the Lord is gra - ci - ous,

Ex. 38 (i)   Locke

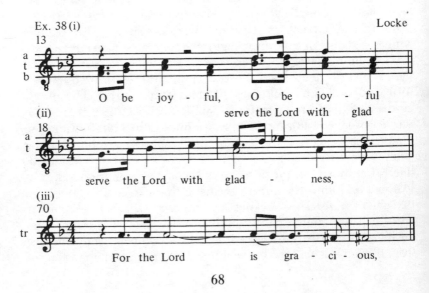

O be joy - ful, O be joy - ful
serve the Lord with glad -

serve the Lord with glad - ness,

For the Lord is gra - ci - ous,

		scoring	bars	t-s	key	
1	Symphony	a4	21	$\frac{3}{4}$	A min	anticipates 2
2	O be joyful	atb	27	$\frac{3}{4}$	A min	
3i	Be ye sure	b	5	$\frac{4}{4}$	A min to E	
ii			21	$\frac{3}{4}$	A min	
4	We are his	TrATB	8	$\frac{3}{4}$	A min	
5	O go your way	ab	20	$\frac{4}{4}$	A min	
6	O be joyful					repeats 2
7i	O be joyful	TrATB	19	$\frac{3}{4}$	A min	based on 2
ii			3	$\frac{4}{4}$		

Total length (excluding 6): 124 bars

FIGURE 5   A Sectional Analysis of Humfrey's anthem *O be joyful*

Locke's sections to be shorter. Humfrey's melodic phrases are longer than Locke's, his internal cadences are fewer, and the development of his ideas is more concentrated and sustained. Humfrey achieves additional coherence through structuring his first two and last two sections on the same thematic material, and through some recurrence of the motive C, D, E, F, D, E, A in the continuo (12.54, 79, 83, 95). These factors suggest that as an adult Humfrey took as his starting point a familiar setting of this text which in its day had been innovative. In reworking some of the same material and adopting one of its formal conventions he was probably intent on outstripping his model, and demonstrating his compositional superiority. A comparison of the two does nevertheless highlight the refinements that the anthem had achieved over a period perhaps as long as a decade, and very largely in Humfrey's own hands.

Humfrey is at his best most consistently in the anthems that set serious texts, and here he marshalled his most powerful resources to create works that were passionate and affecting. *Lord teach us to number our days*, amounting to 158 bars, is among the shortest, but like the others in this category, its tightly-knit structure contributes to its concentration of expression. There are comparatively few internal sections, and these merge one into another (11.56) aided by the smooth integration of their constituent textures (11.117 and 125). The anthem is further unified first by the descending motive D, C, B, A, G sharp in continuo and vocal lines

(11.43, 115, 130, 153), and by slightly modified forms of this motive (11.5, 30, 92, 123, 139, 147, 154). A second unifying motive is the interval of a falling fourth which is prominent in some of the anthem's most expressive episodes.

The falling fourth is a predominant factor in the striking correspondences that exist between the opening of the first verse of this anthem (Ex. 39(i)), and those of Locke's *Lord let me know my end*[4] (Ex. 39(ii)), and Blow's *Lord how are they increased*[5] (Ex. 39(iii)). Each is in A minor and begins with tenor soloist and continuo. Discounting octave transpositions, the intervallic organization of the continuo line of all three is identical. The differences in rhythmic organization between Humfrey on one hand, and Locke and Blow on the other, arise from the continuo's imitative integration with the tenor line in Locke and Blow which is symptomatic of their more innate inclination towards imitative counterpoint. Such integration is much less characteristic of Humfrey. The tenor lines of Locke and Blow also begin identically in interval, and are characteristically more disjunct than Humfrey's opening melody. Even towards the end of his life, Locke remained a comparatively eclectic composer, and as *Lord let me know my end* is uniformly in the affective style, the vogue for which was created largely by Humfrey, I would suggest that it was influenced by Humfrey's work in general and probably by *Lord teach us to number our days* in particular. Blow's *Lord how are they increased* was composed by 1676, and would seem to present a clearer case of a direct borrowing from Locke, perhaps to begin an essay in a style that Blow was thus seeking to master. Locke's excursion into the affective style with a possible debt to some of Humfrey's material may even have prompted Humfrey to respond in like manner by taking Locke's *O be joyful* as a starting point for his own setting. Whatever the precise reasons for these correspondences, the attraction of Locke to the affective style at the end of his life, and of Blow towards the beginning of his, attests to the strength of Humfrey's influence over his greatest English contemporaries.

Hear my crying O God, spanning 276 bars, is Humfrey's most extensive anthem, and its inner proportions are correspondingly lavish. It has five substantial ritornellos, all developing material from the preceding verse, as does the final chorus. Apart from a treble solo punctuated by a solo violin (5.85), its verses are all ensembles, and the last (5.197) contains Humfrey's only five-part

Ex. 39 (i)   Humfrey
11.41

Lord   teach   us   to   num - ber our days

(ii)   Locke

Lord,   let me know   my   end,

(iii)   Blow

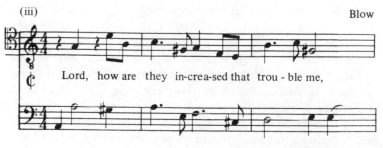

Lord, how are they in-crea-sed that trou - ble me,

US - Aus, Gostling MS, p. 43, rear

writing. All sections except its central verse remain in A minor, but this more complex structure moves to a central section in C major.

The remaining three anthems in the affective vein represent Humfrey's finest work, and are among the small masterpieces of the period. *Like as the hart* sets a text concerned largely with gentle aspirations, and Humfrey responded with rising conjunct phrases and leaps to an extent that is unusual in his style. Almost every section contains, for example, prominent rising fourths. The number of internal sections is comparatively few despite the anthem's length of 163 bars, and a group of these (10.40–123), accounting for over half the anthem, move from the tonic of F minor to a tonal centre of C minor. Nowhere else does Humfrey make such prolonged tonal excursion.

Of all Humfrey's anthems, *By the waters of Babylon* is the most overtly dramatic. The weight of oppression experienced by the exiled Jews is given a vivid immediacy by the falling patterns which pervade melody and harmony throughout the anthem. One of the less apparent but no less powerful instances underpins the ttb verse setting 'and melody in our heaviness' (2.60–7) where for eight bars the continuo line descends in near-conjunct movement and with octave transpositions for one note short of two octaves. Even this structural application of the pervasive pattern can contribute to the uniformity of mood within the anthem.

Alone among the adult anthems, the string movements of *By the waters of Babylon* are in only three parts. Perhaps because of the serious nature of its opening text, the first symphony contains only the duple section. As in *Like as the hart* and *O Lord my God* which also begin with only a duple symphony, there is a substantial triple-time symphony about the centre of the anthem which compensates for its earlier omission. Each of the ritornellos of *By the waters of Babylon* takes up material from the preceding verse, but in a manner far removed from the conventional echo ritornello of Cooke. Each of Humfrey's ritornellos reinforces and sustains the dramatic mood created by the verse.

The most dramatic episode in this, or any other anthem by Humfrey, pits the jeering Babylonians against the lamenting Jews (2.71–102) in a musical language that draws on the most powerful and contrasting resources at his disposal. The chorus representing the Babylonians sing in triple time and in a homophony which veers considerably towards flatter keys from the F minor tonic, all suggesting the oppressiveness of the captors. The response from the Jews represented by ttb verse is made in duple time, and contains Humfrey's most bitterly chromatic counterpoint. In the second of their two exchanges (Ex. 40), the verse singers weave from bar 85 lines of extreme angularity, creating progressions of harsh dissonance which lend a particular immediacy to their

Ex. 40

plaint. The continuo initially rises carrying the texture through chromatic notes sharp of the tonic, but from bar 88 it progressively falls leading the verse singers through the darker spectrum of flatter keys.

O Lord my God is arguably Humfrey's finest single work. Behind its sustained emotional immediacy there lies one of Humfrey's most cogently organized structures which contributes significantly to the anthem's expressive concentration. Coherence is achieved equally through tonal and motivic means. Of its ten sections, the six up to and including the central repetition of the opening symphony are in the tonic of the anthem, F minor, and each has a prominent internal move to a related key. The seventh, eighth, and ninth sections, however, constitute a broader ternary paragraph which moves to a tonal centre of C minor before returning to F minor for the final repetition of the single chorus. Humfrey's grasp of contemporary Italian principles of tonal organization is illustrated further by an episode within the first symphony which is built over a sequence of slowly moving falling fifths in the bass (14.6–8). *O Lord my God* contains Humfrey's most thorough application of motivic unification, and the four-note descending phrase, F, E flat, D flat, C, with which the bass soloist begins the first verse (14.12–13), is found in the continuo line of every section of the anthem (see Ex. 41 and also 14.43–5, 60–2, 65–6, 95–6); where the tonal centre moves to C minor, the motive begins on C (14.119–22). One note of the motive can be transposed by an octave (14.4–5), and in one statement an extra semitone can be added (14.17–18), without distorting its identity in any way. The motive usually unfolds in minims, but in the triple-time chorus each note can account basically for one bar (14.79–82), and at the beginning of the verse 'For many dogs are come about me' it unfolds more slowly and irregularly over an elongated span of five bars, and thus contributes to the bleak mood of the text (14.102–6).

Each of the first two verses, a bass arioso and an alto and tenor duet, achieves a cumulative emotional immediacy by progressing from a comparatively lyrical style to a starker declamation. The central chorus, which is repeated at the end of the anthem, and the final verse share one phrase in common (14.79 and 149). In each instance Humfrey develops the phrase into an episode of mounting tension by means of a chain of suspended dissonances which unfold over the recurrent motive (Ex. 41). Such dissonance had its origins in the finest music of the *seconda prattica*, and characterized, for example, the setting of 'Sacrificium Deo' in Lully's *Miserere mei Deus*.[6] *O Lord my God* encapsulates the finest distillations which Humfrey made from contemporary Italian and French styles, and demonstrates the artistry with which he was able to graft these into a distinctive style of his own which was fashioned to meet English circumstances.

Humfrey's setting of the service could hardly be further

removed from the emotive style of the finest verse anthems. In common with other Restoration services, his setting represents not so much an expressive response to details of the text as a vehicle for the impersonal grandeur of the liturgy. Comprising the two morning canticles and the two evening canticles, together with the maximum number of sections of the communion service then sung, it is among the most complete services of its period. It adopts the style of the traditional English short service, being basically syllabic in texture and employing recurrent thematic material. As became common in Restoration services, episodes for full chorus contrast with ensemble verses in three or four parts, and the whole texture is accompanied by the organ which almost exclusively doubles the voice parts. Its harmonic vocabulary is distinctively Humfrey's, although, largely divorced from the expressive contexts from which this arose, it can seem mannered. Humfrey's single chant is in the same impersonal style, and is distinctive only for its being included in what is probably the earliest collection of 'Tunes in foure parts to the Psalms of David' dating from 1676.[7]

V

THE COURT ODES

No proud seventeenth-century court considered itself complete without the lustre that music provided, and after the Restoration in England the two principal secular festivals of the year, New Year's Day and the birthday of Charles II on 29 May, came to be celebrated with elaborate odes. The impetus behind these festivals came largely from the masque tradition at the court of Charles I, and the sumptuous entertainments that Charles II had enjoyed at the French court in the early years of his exile. Appropriating characteristics from both, the Restoration court ode became an entertainment that revolved around a glorification of the King expressed in music which was closely associated with courtly dancing. Given the nature of their stylistic models and of the music itself, it is not unlikely that the odes or sections of them were actually danced by the courtiers. From the beginning of the Restoration composers cast their odes in the grandest form that was most readily at hand, that of the verse anthem with strings, and where they deviated from its conventions, they did so to accommodate more prominent elements of the dance.

The earliest extant Restoration ode dates from 1664, and from the following decade seven odes survive complete, one by Locke and three each by Cooke and Humfrey. The texts of two others have survived, one by Lanier and one by Locke.[1] The three by Humfrey are the last of this group, and being considerably more extensive than any of the others, they attest to the growing individuality of the form. Dating from comparatively late in his short career, each takes as its starting point the proportions of his grander verse anthems. His first ode, *See mighty Sir*, celebrated New Year's Day in 1672, his next, *When from his throne*, was written for the King's birthday in the same year,[2] and both set texts by his friend Robert Veel (1648–?74). His third ode, *Smile smile again* (author unknown), can be conjecturally assigned to the King's birthday in 1673.

Of Humfrey's three odes, *Smile smile again* is furthest removed in design from the conventions of the verse anthem, but most of its deviations are found to some degree in one or both of the other odes. The structural analysis of *Smile smile again* (Fig. 6) immediately discloses a higher proportion of exact repetition than is found in the verse anthems. Its symphony is repeated at three subsequent points, and its opening verse is repeated twice. The material of this verse is repeated immediately by the chorus, section 3, and that chorus is also repeated twice subsequently. The second and third solo verses, sections 5 and 9, are each followed by ritornellos which take up material from the end of the verses. In each of the odes there is a far greater incidence of solo verses than is found in the anthems, and most of these consist of two or three internal divisions each with a contrast of metre. In both *Smile smile again* and *When from his throne* there are substantial solo verses for all four voices. The sections that make up the odes are all of considerable length, but all begin and end in the tonic. There are

		scoring	bars	t-s	key	
1i	Symphony	a4	13	$\frac{4}{4}$	E min	
ii			24	$\frac{3}{4}$	E min	traces of 2
2	Smile smile again	tr	22	$\frac{3}{4}$	E min	
3	Smile smile again	TrATB	23	$\frac{3}{4}$	E min	repeats 2
4	Symphony					repeats 1
5i	Thou mighty sabbath	b	7	$\frac{4}{4}$	E min to G	
ii			12	$\frac{3}{4}$	G to E min	
iii		a	12	$\frac{6}{4}$ 6i	E min	Ex. 43
6	Ritornello	a4	3	$\frac{6}{4}$ 6i	E min	repeats 5iii
7	This day gave	atb	12	$\frac{6}{4}$ 6i	E min	based on 5iii
8	Smile smile again					repeats 2, 3, 1
9i	See see how every	t	7	$\frac{4}{4}$	E min to G	
ii			16	$\frac{2}{2}$ ₵	E min	
10	Ritornello	a4	17	$\frac{2}{2}$ ₵	E min	based on 9ii
11i	Thrice happy morn	b	8	$\frac{3}{4}$	E min to B	
ii			8	$\frac{4}{4}$	B to G maj	
iii		atb	31	$\frac{3}{4}$	G to E min	
12	Symphony					repeats 1, 2, 3
	Smile smile again					

Total length (excluding 4, 8, and 12): 215 bars

FIGURE 6 A Sectional Analysis of Humfrey's ode *Smile smile again*

77

none of the broader ternary tonal structures that characterize some of the verse anthems. Each of the odes contains at least one recurrent thematic motive which adds further unity to that provided by the exact repetition of sections.

Major stylistic differences between the odes and the verse anthems originate in the differences in the form and content of their texts. The texts of the odes are metrical and consist largely of sycophantic doggerel, and they have almost none of the propulsive irregularity and fertile imagery of the prose texts from the bible which resulted in such expressive settings in the verse anthems. Occasionally Humfrey seized on a particular word for illustrative concentration, but any emphasis on emotive expression would have been wholly out of place in these courtly celebrations, and their vocal style is predominantly lyrical in both duple and triple time. The essential individuality of the odes stems from their wholesale appropriation of French courtly dance measures.

Each of the odes begins with a complete symphony, and the triple section of each is as long as, and in *When from his throne* considerably longer than, the most extensive triple sections of the symphonies in the verse anthems. Such emphasis at the very least accentuates the origins of this triple section in the contemporary French sarabande, and as part of a secular ode, these movements may actually have been danced. This may account for the multiple repetitions of the symphonies in the later odes. Most of the ritornellos in the odes repeat the material and consequently the metre of the end of the preceding verse. Each of the two more independent ritornellos in the odes adopts the patterns of the French sarabande (21.65, 23.199).

In two of the odes, Humfrey introduces into vocal textures two time-signatures and consequential rhythmic conventions that are specifically associated with French courtly dances, and that are wholly absent from the verse anthems. Section 9 and its ritornello section 10 in *Smile smile again* employ the faster time-signature $\oint$. Humfrey's association of this with a specific dance is confirmed by the tenor verse 'The days are all at loyal strife' in *See mighty Sir* with a time-signature of $\oint$ which he actually designated 'Gavot' (Ex. 42). *Smile smile again* is the only ode to employ the time-signature 6i, and although not so named, these episodes unequivocally adopt the conventions of the jig. This dance had as strong an ancestry in English music as it had in French (Ex. 43).

In each of the odes Humfrey employed hemiola phrases in both

Gavot

t

The days are all at loy - al strife,

bc

76

t

which shall be'the hap - piest of your life, and

bc

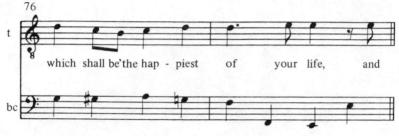

Ex. 43
22.101

a

6i Let him dance while we sing joy and health to our king,

bc

airs and choruses to an extent far greater than the occasional hemiolas that cluster about cadences in the verse anthems. The basic pattern involves the interpolation of one phrase in $\frac{3}{2}$, ♩·♪♩♩♩·♪, alternating with one or two bars in $\frac{3}{4}$ within a section in $\frac{3}{4}$. These characteristics are the basis of yet another dance of French origin, the courante, and these sections in the odes may also have been danced at the English court. The courante is only tentatively suggested in *See mighty Sir* (21.50 and 84), and here verbal and harmonic stress do not always coincide. In the later odes, however, it is used more pervasively and with greater assurance, and throughout two groups of sections in *When from his throne*, beginning with the airs 'The wat'ry gods' and 'Your gracious bounty', one phrase in $\frac{3}{2}$ alternates with one or two in $\frac{3}{4}$ with a prevalence of the courante's rhythmic conventions (Ex. 44, and 23.123).

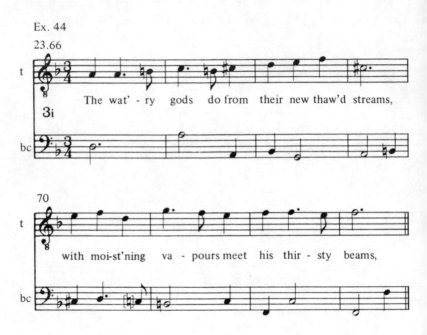

Ex. 44

23.66

Humfrey's first ode, *See mighty Sir*, is closest in style to the verse anthem. A number of its episodes employ the time-signature ₵ including the tenor solo marked 'Gavot', but none uses the time-signature 6i. Unlike the later odes, its symphony is played only at the beginning. Two of its three substantial solo verses are scored for tenor, and were doubtless designed to bring Humfrey before the King in his first ode as both composer and singer. The thematic material on which the triple sections of the final verse and chorus are built (21.179 and 210), and which sets the words 'So shall we always sing thanks', is almost identical to the principal material of the final verse and chorus of *Hear my crying O God*, which sets the words 'So will I alway sing praise' (5.210 and 253). Both episodes are in triple time, and both are propelled by Humfrey's distinctive striding bass. The development of the material is more extensive in the anthem which suggests that it may post-date the ode.

From the modest odes by Cooke and Locke, Humfrey created a vehicle for a lavish aristocratic entertainment which revolved about a glorification of the King, and celebrated the stability which he personified. In Humfrey's hands the ode achieved a distinctive identity which illuminates aspects of his own creativity wholly different from those of the verse anthems, and which laid the foundation for further expansions of the form in the next generation by Blow and Purcell.

VI

THE SONGS

DURING the Commonwealth, the singing of songs had been one of the most widespread forms of music-making, and although after the Restoration it was overshadowed by more spectacular music, it lost none of its former popularity. Songs were in demand at court in organized entertainments or in more impromptu circumstances; they became an integral component of Restoration theatre, and they were widely performed in the homes of eager amateurs. Initially they circulated in manuscript collections made by enthusiasts like Edward Lowe of Oxford, but from the early 1670s collections of songs began to be more widely disseminated in print. These met an increasing demand for the latest songs in vogue, and the first edition of John Playford's *Choice Songs and Ayres* (1673) proudly claimed to offer 'Most of the Newest Songs sung at *Court*, and at the Publick Theatres'. The addition of new songs in each of Playford's six subsequent editions published to 1684 attests to the growing popularity of this Restoration miniature.

Furthermore, despite its comparatively modest design, the song became a medium which clearly reflected subtle changes in musical taste in the first generation of the Restoration, changes which were slower to surface in more elaborate forms.[1] As in other spheres of music, the French taste of Charles II was decisive in the development of the song. Roger North maintained that the King

approved onely the soft vein, such as might be called a step tripla, and that made a fashion among the masters, and for the stage, as may be seen in the printed books of the songs of that time.[2]

In the first decade of the Restoration, there was an overwhelming vogue for the triple-time lyric, and like the court ode, this fell under the dominant influence of French dance measures as North confirmed. The form and content of these triple-time songs were so little determined by the text set that they are in essence dance music with words. With the ascendancy of the triple-time lyric, the older declamatory ayre in duple time with its values of emotive arioso fell from general favour. By the early 1670s it began to be

replaced by the robust duple-time ballad whose musical symmetries and uncomplicated lyricism reflected the prevailing values
of the triple-time lyric.

It is probable that the majority of Humfrey's twenty-seven or
twenty-eight songs were composed by 1672. Eleven of his secular
songs were included in Playford's *Choice Songs and Ayres* (1673),
and the texts of fifteen were printed in 1671 and 1672. As the
collections of texts stress that they include the newest songs sung
at court and in the theatres, it is probable that the composition of
the song preceded the publication of its text. All of Humfrey's
songs set metrical texts, and their subject matter falls into four
principal categories: bawdy lyrics, love laments, dramatic episodes, and devotional songs. Two of the secular songs were written
for revels at court. *I pass all my hours in a shady old grove*, whose
text was supposedly by Charles II, was described as 'The first
Song in the Ball at Court', and *A lover I'm born and a lover I'll be* as
'A second Song in the Masque at Court'.[3] Both were probably part
of the grand ballet which was danced at court on 20 February
1671, and which was celebrated for its fine music and excellent
new songs.[4] The text of *How well doth this harmonious meeting
prove* was described by Robert Veel as 'A Song *in Commendation of
an Annual* Musick-Meeting',[5] and Humfrey's second setting of
this text was described as 'A Song *Sung at a* Musick *Feast*'.[6] These
songs were probably written for the annual gathering of The
Musical Society in the city which from 1683 grew into the more
formal St Cecilia's Day celebration.

At least five of Humfrey's songs were composed for plays in the
city. *Cheer up my mates* was written for one of the revivals of
Fletcher and Massinger's *The Sea Voyage* in March or May 1668.
Hark hark hark the storm grows loud was also written for this play.
It is the first song in Playford's *Choice Songs and Ayres* (1673)
where it was ascribed to Robert Smith, but as the next two songs
are by Humfrey, and in the two subsequent editions of Playford,
Smith's name was deleted, this ascription may be incorrect. The
song is found twice in one contemporary manuscript, first in the
hand of Matthew Locke and unascribed, but the second copy
ascribes it to Humfrey.[7] It is a powerful declamatory air in duple
time throughout with sufficient imprints of Humfrey's musical
and dramatic style to make his authorship probable. *Ah fading joy*
was composed for Dryden's *The Indian Emperour* produced in
January 1668, and *Wherever I am or whatever I do* for Dryden's

The Conquest of Granada which opened about December 1670. *A wife I do hate* was written for Wycherley's *Love in a Wood* produced at the Theatre Royal in March 1671, and *O love if e'er thou'lt ease a heart* for Crowne's *The History of Charles the Eighth of France* staged at the new Dorset Garden Theatre late in November 1671.

Although Humfrey's songs for the theatre include some of his most elaborate settings, they also include simple lyrics, and there is no consistent correlation between the provenance of a song and its musical style. In fact the essence of Humfrey's secular songs lies in neither their provenance nor their subject matter, but in their musical symmetries and their relation to contemporary courtly dances. His lyrical songs are characterized by shapely melodies, and by regular phrase lengths determined by their metrical texts without repetition of words, and by regular cadences. Much of the appeal of these songs is concentrated in their melodies. These regularly employ Humfrey's distinctive melodic imprints, and they introduce rhythmic patterns derived from the dance. On the other hand, the songs adopt almost none of the emotive chromatic harmony which had distinguished the verse anthems. The cadences of the songs disclose a carefully devised tonal organization, particularly in the songs in minor keys, beginning in the tonic and moving through related keys before returning to the tonic. The longer the song, the more distant the tonal excursions as defined by the internal cadences. Twelve of Humfrey's songs are strophic, and in another seven his setting of a strophic text spans at least two stanzas. In most of the latter, his settings are virtually, if not actually, through-composed.

The largest category of Humfrey's songs is the simple lyrics in triple time. All twelve are secular, and all but one are strophic. As that single exception, *Though you doom all to die*, survives in a single, early nineteenth-century source which did not include additional stanzas, it too may have been strophic originally. It is in the triple-time lyrics and in other songs with sections in triple time that the influence of the dance is most pronounced. The time-signature of the majority of these is $\frac{3}{4}$ (originally C3) which together with their rhythmic patterns establishes an immediate affinity with the contemporary French sarabande. The form of the rhythmic pattern that is most common in the songs places the stress on the first beat of each bar, and only occasionally is the stress placed on the second beat. Never in the songs is there any consistent alternation of stress between the second beat of one bar and the first beat of the next, as characterized more the complex form of the sarabande found in Humfrey's verse anthems and court odes. The most elaborate application of sarabande rhythmic patterns is found in Humfrey's longest song (76 bars), *Thus Cupid commences his rapes and vagaries*, where the second beat is stressed throughout the first line, and from the third line the first beat is stressed except towards strategic cadence points (Ex. 45). This example illustrates the regularity of the phrase lengths, and the progressive deviation of its frequent cadences from the tonic of C minor such as characterizes the longer songs.

Two of the triple-time songs, *A wife I do hate* and *Let fortune and Phillis frown if they please*, sustain the rhythmic and harmonic organization of the jig, although their original time-signatures in the printed sources do not differ from those of the sarabandes (Ex. 46). Their harmonic rhythm is slower, their phrases are longer, and feminine endings are more prevalent than in other triple-time lyrics. There is no consistent appropriation of the courante in any of the songs although there is a single instance of its two-bar hemiola pattern in the first setting of *How well doth this harmonious meeting prove* (32a.11).

Although there are only five secular songs by Humfrey in duple time, their style is considerably more diverse than that of any of his own triple-time lyrics, or any of the duple-time songs by his contemporaries. While in the work of the latter the emotive style of the declamatory ayre had been almost totally eclipsed by the triple-time lyric, Humfrey could still put to affective use variable phrase lengths and harmonic rhythm, angular melodies and starker declamation, and rests which expressively punctuate melodic lines. Elsewhere, and sometimes within the same song, he could abandon this style for the more symmetrical lyricism of the newer duple-time ballad. In none of Humfrey's duple-time songs is there any trace whatever of the influence of dance measures. The only contemporary suggestion of any relation between duple-time song and the dance lies in William Gregory's description of one of his own songs as an 'Almain'.[8] But neither this nor any other English duple-time song of the day has any genuine affinity with the almain, and such a designation reflects more probably Gregory's attempt to conform to a contemporary vogue.

Of Humfrey's five secular songs in duple time, one is through-composed, two are partially strophic, and two wholly strophic. *As*

42.1

Thus Cu - pid com - men - ces his rapes and va-ga - ries, And sports him - self with fe - male pas-sions; A thou - sand times o - ver he chan - ges and va - ries, their fan - cies as oft as their fash-ions:

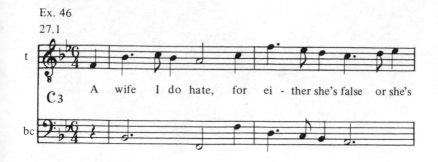

freezing fountains, the single through-composed duple-time song, begins as a ballad with a symmetrical phrase structure; the music of lines 1 to 4 is remoulded to set lines 5 to 8, and there is no repetition of words and almost no use of rests. This half of the poem deals in conventional pastorale similes, but at the mid-point where the poet turns more directly to his own despair, Humfrey turns to a more impassioned style derived from arioso with a repetition of 'such' following rests on successive strong beats, and an intensifying melisma on 'absence'. Ex. 47, consisting of lines 5 to 9 of the poem, illustrates Humfrey's expressive transition from one style to the other, occasioned by the content of the poem. The two partially strophic duple-time secular songs, *Oh that I had but a fine man* and *Phillis for shame let us improve* are almost wholly ballad-like although the former concludes with one phrase of arioso (38.11–14) to express the singer's ultimate despair. Each of the two wholly strophic songs in this category, *O love if e'er thou'lt ease a heart* and *When Aurelia first I courted,* is uniformly in the lyrical ballad style, and differs from the triple-time lyric only in metre. The second is one of two songs (the other is *Thus Cupid commences his rapes and vagaries*) which was published initially in

87

Ex. 47

or as a hope-less droop - ing flower for day de-par-ted grieves, possessed of nothing but a shower of tears u - pon her leaves. Such, such am I in your ab - sence left,

Choice Songs and Ayres (1673) as a solo song, but which in *Choice Ayres, Songs, & Dialogues* (1675) became duets. In each case the continuo line was slightly modified to become a bass vocal line, but this constituted no real change to the original design of either song.

Multi-sectional songs were rare in the output of Humfrey's contemporaries, but he himself more frequently built extended songs from a number of sections contrasting duple and triple metres together with their attendant stylistic distinctions. The duple-triple bipartite structure had originated in the Italian *seconda prattica*, and Humfrey adopted it pervasively throughout his output. The duple section of the bipartite *Cupid once when weary grown* fluctuates expressively between the lyrical and the more dramatically declamatory. The resolution of tensions narrated by the text is matched by a resolution into triple time (30.26), in which Humfrey achieves a fine reconciliation between lyricism and his distinctive species of sinuously chromatic melody.[9] *Cheer up my mates*, a song designed for the theatre, alternates duple and triple sections twice, and although the former are only short, they are overtly dramatic. In the second duple section, for example, 'Hey boys, she scudds away' prompts a flamboyant and rapid descending octave scale (29.17–19). In each of his settings of *How well doth this harmonious meeting prove*, Humfrey added to his bipartite song a final three-part chorus. Such three-part refrain choruses may have originated in French dramatic music, and were to recur in Humfrey's two masques in *The Tempest*. Humfrey's most complex song, *Ah fading joy* dating from 1668, is probably one of his earliest. It alternates duple and triple sections twice, and the duples range expressively from the lyrical to the declamatory; it concludes with a three-part chorus which is itself bipartite.[10]

In the five devotional songs, Humfrey returned to texts expressing intimate spiritual feelings, and these drew from him settings which return to the affective musical language of his finest verse anthems. Four of the five consistently employ the emotive arioso which had dominated the anthems but which had been overshadowed in the secular songs by lyrical symmetries and dance measures. There is no trace whatever of the dance in the devotional songs. Four are wholly in duple time, and the triple section of the bipartite *Sleep downy sleep come close mine eyes* is smoothly lyrical and conspicuously avoids any suggestion of dance-like rhythms.

Hark how the wakeful cheerful cock, described in *Harmonia Sacra* I (1688) as 'A Dialogue between two Penitents', is the only wholly dramatic song and the only duet among the devotional songs. A note in its near-contemporary manuscript source added that it was 'Begun By Mr. Humphreis, and finishd by Dr. John Blow'.[11] The exchanges between the two penitents, accounting for 91 bars, are probably all by Humfrey, and the final 22-bar chorus for alto, tenor, and continuo is probably by Blow. The former adopt an uncompromisingly declamatory style throughout with lines abounding in falling diminished intervals, rapidly repeated notes, rests, and abrupt interjections. These all intensify the growing remorse of the penitents, and give the song a heightened, if rather exaggerated, immediacy which is lacking from most of the secular laments. The final chorus is built from a succession of disjunct points of imitation which sustain the type of contrapuntal texture that was foreign to Humfrey.

Lord I have sinned is a through-composed setting of two stanzas of verse in emotive arioso, and its expressive weight falls on the melody. Chromatic alteration and falling diminished intervals are plentiful, and Humfrey goes as far as isolating the words 'run', 'drops', 'laughter', and 'melt' in bars 10, 12, 29, and 33 for species of word-painting which are generally absent from the anthems. Although this song is through-composed, its second stanza does return to some of the most distinctive gestures of the first, and of these four words, 'laughter' and 'melt' take their cue respectively from the setting of 'run' and 'drops'. The final lines of the song (Ex. 48) illustrate the expressive demands which Humfrey makes on his melody, demands which exceed any found in the verse anthems and verge on the exaggerated. The sinuous chromaticism and extravagant leaps stand in marked contrast to the simple harmonic basis which moves from a penultimate cadence in B flat to the final tonic of G minor.

O the sad day is another semi-dramatic song cast in the emotive declamatory style of the arioso. Like others in this category, despite its metrical text, the variable phrase lengths, repetitions of words, and melismas all preclude any symmetrical regularity which the text might otherwise have imposed. The only purely lyrical devotional song is *Sleep downy sleep come close mine eyes*, and being bipartite, it is the only devotional song to venture into triple time. Each section is made up of a cumulative succession of short, regular phrases, and the modest melodic intensifications of the song are all contained within a rigorously controlled symmetry. The poem, by an unknown author, is rich in simple images, and Humfrey responded with one of his most beguiling simple songs.

John Donne's *A Hymn to God the Father, Wilt thou forgive that sin*, is the finest poem that Humfrey set, and it drew from him the most intricately structured and expressive of all his songs. Donne's *Hymn* is preoccupied with his own pilgrimage towards salvation to the extent that each of its three stanzas culminates in a pun on the word 'done'. Humfrey seized on this concentration, and although his setting is superficially through-composed, significant phrases

Ex. 48

46.31

Teach but my   heart and eyes   to   melt   a -

- way,   and then   one   drop,   one   drop of

bal - som   will   suf - fice.

in the poem's second and third stanzas spring from the cor-
responding line in the first stanza. The opening of each stanza
(Ex. 49) illustrates just such a derivation of the second and third
from the first, and the resultant musical and expressive concentration. The second stanza begins a fifth higher than the first and is
effortlessly extended; from the third of the scale the third stanza
rises to a higher pitch and is also extended by a bar. The final
couplet of the song (see Ex. 12) also expands the ends of the first
two stanzas with some of the most expressive gestures at Humfrey's command. Although the *Hymn* maintains the style of the

49.1

(ii)

49.13

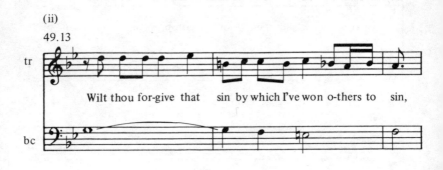

(iii)

49.24

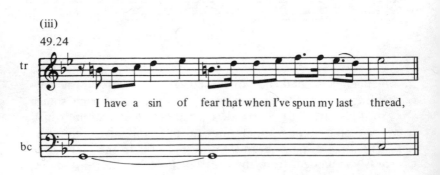

arioso at its most lyrical, the weight of expression still falls on its melody. Unlike *Lord I have sinned*, however, whose sentiments and style are superficially similar, there are no melodic exaggerations in *Wilt thou forgive that sin*, and its intensity is a product of its finely calculated cumulative concentration. Such concentration perfectly matches that of Donne's *Hymn*, and in this most technically disciplined of all his songs, Humfrey created one of the most expressive miniatures of the entire Restoration period.

VII

THE MUSIC FOR *THE TEMPEST*

AFTER the ban on public theatres imposed during the Commonwealth, the restoration of Charles II witnessed a burgeoning of
theatrical entertainments both at court and in the city. Before the
end of 1660 two companies had been formed and granted official
patents. The King's Company under Thomas Killigrew played in
successive theatres in Drury Lane. The more powerful and
significant Duke of York's Company was founded by William
Davenant, and played first in the Lincoln's Inn Fields Theatre and
from 1671 in a new theatre in Dorset Garden. Throughout its two
decades the Duke's Company maintained a strong French bias
thus reinforcing the vogue so actively encouraged by Charles II.

Davenant was the Restoration's principal link with Caroline
theatrical traditions. In the previous reign he had written four
court masques in which music, dancing, and spectacle had played
a prominent part. During the Civil War and until 1650, he had
lived mainly in Paris where he was in regular contact with the
English royal exiles, Henrietta Maria and Charles. It is likely that
in their company he would have seen some of the Italian
entertainments that Cardinal Mazarin was then introducing to a
reluctant French court. While in Paris he must also have seen the
tragédies à machines which were currently in fashion at the *Théâtre
du Marais*. These were heroic plays interspersed with music and
dancing, but their most novel attraction was their use of elaborate
machines for spectacle. It was the intention of Corneille, whose
Andromède (1650) was one of the most popular of the type, that
nothing essential to the plot should be sung.[1] Davenant's two most
ambitious productions for the Restoration stage were his adap-
tations of *Macbeth* and *The Tempest*, and both assert the powerful
influence of these two foreign models against the backcloth of the
Caroline courtly masque.

Macbeth opened at the Lincoln's Inn Fields Theatre in
November 1664 and played regularly for the remainder of the
decade. In February 1673 it was revived at the Dorset Garden

94

Theatre in a new production which added elaborate spectacle that was made possible by the technical resources of the new theatre. The music for the original production was by Matthew Locke, but of this only two simple dances have survived.[2]

Prompted no doubt by the success of *Macbeth*, Davenant, in collaboration with John Dryden, made an adaptation of *The Tempest* for the Duke's Company, and this opened at the Lincoln's Inn Fields Theatre on 7 November 1667. In his Preface to the quarto published in 1670, Dryden attributed the adaptation basically to Davenant. The rationale behind the simplifications, excisions, and additions made to Shakespeare's play encapsulate much of the distinctive aesthetic of the Restoration theatre. Shakespeare's plot was simplified and much of his language was compressed as the Restoration sought to clothe its drama rather less in verbal subtleties than in sensual and scenic impact. As was explained in the Prologue to a production of Shirley's *Love Tricks*, also dating from 1667,

> That which the World call'd Wit in *Shakespeare's* Age
> Is laught at, as improper for our Stage.[3]

Characters of the opposite sex were added to complement Shakespeare's characters in order that, as Dryden's Preface put it, 'Innocence and Love might the more illustrate and commend each other'. The most significant additions, however, lie in the expansions of spectacle and the supernatural, and both were portrayed principally through further singing and dancing introduced into what was already Shakespeare's most musical play. In the tradition of the *tragédie à machines*, no major character sang, but in the most substantial addition, *The Masque of the Two Devils* in Act II, supernatural and allegorical figures upbraid some of the principal characters for their crimes of usurpation.

Dryden and Davenant retained most of Shakespeare's songs, but changed either their positions or their singers (see Fig. 7). The only music to have survived from this production are four songs by John Banister, *Come unto these yellow sands*, *Full fathom five*, *Dry those eyes*, and Ferdinand and Ariel's echo song, *Go thy way*, and these almost certainly did so because they were retained in the later production of the play. That they originated in the 1667 production is confirmed by Pepys who attended no fewer than nine performances, and on three of these he mentioned the music.

95

On the opening night he was particularly intrigued by Ferdinand and Ariel's echo song in Act III, and his description of it matches Banister's setting exactly. Later in the season, on 11 May 1668, his curiosity got the better of him, and he went backstage after the performance to get Henry Harris, who had played Ferdinand, to repeat the words for him. Furthermore, as Pepys, who was a keen commentator on Pelham Humfrey's progress after the latter's return from France in October 1667, made no mention of Humfrey in connection with the 1667 production, it can be assumed with some confidence that Humfrey made no contribution to it. Eighteen performances of *The Tempest* are recorded between November 1667 and its final night on 14 November 1670, and its popularity must have prompted the Duke's Company to consider a new production which would involve even more lavish resources.

Meanwhile in 1668 William Davenant died, and the Restoration theatre lost its most experienced link with French practice. The management of the Duke's Company passed to Thomas Betterton and Henry Harris, and soon it became apparent that Betterton would not only maintain, but reinforce the French bias that Davenant had established in the Duke's Company. To cater for the French-inspired vogue for productions involving more spectacular scenes and machines, the Company moved in November 1671 to a new theatre in Dorset Garden designed by Sir Christopher Wren specifically to accommodate the most elaborate spectacle.

The most recent French courtly entertainments were forging a closer integration of music and drama. Lully's *comédies-ballets* had been gradually developing in this direction since 1663, and in 1671 he was on the threshold of taking such integration into the more intrinsically dramatic medium of opera. Although English theatrical taste preferred to maintain a separation of the essentials of the plot and any music, there is some evidence that this separation became eroded as the Restoration progressed. Robert Stapylton's *The Step-mother* (October 1663) and Elkanah Settle's *The Empress of Morocco* (1673), both contain masques in which the drama reaches some species of climax; significantly the music of the masques in both plays was by Locke.[4] *The Masque of the Two Devils* in Act II of *The Tempest* (1667) had, in a minor way, also served to reinforce a perception of the dramatic oppositions at work. Thus by the early 1670s, the London stage was prepared for a more spectacular species of theatre, and one which could sustain some closer alliance of music and plot.

1674 was an active year for the London theatre. On 30 March the King's Company opened the French opera *Ariane ou le Mariage de Baccus* by Perrin and Cambert with additions by Grabu. The Duke's Company responded on 30 April with a new production of *The Tempest*.[5] The title page of its quarto, published in 1674, read *The Tempest or The Enchanted Isle*, but there was no mention of the author or the adapter. However the Company's prompter, John Downes, described the production as 'The Tempest, or the Inchanted Island, made into an Opera by *Mr. Shadwell*',[6] and in the absence of any stronger evidence to the contrary, this would appear to confirm that Thomas Shadwell was indeed the adapter.

Shadwell took the earlier adaptation by Dryden and Davenant as his starting point. His innovations were all designed to expand the elements of the supernatural and spectacle made possible by the new mechanical resources of the Dorset Garden Theatre, and to this end he introduced a significant expansion of vocal and instrumental music, and dancing (see Figs. 7 and 8). In his epilogue for *The Tempest* of 1674, Shadwell confirmed the importance of these elements in his scheme, and made his identification with the French tradition that had been initiated by Davenant explicit.

> From [France] new Arts to please you, we have sought
> We have machines to some perfection brought,
> And above 30 Warbling voyces gott.
> Many a God & Goddesse you will heare
> And we have Singing, Dancing, Devills here
> Such Devills, and such gods, are very Deare.[7]

Banister's four songs were retained from the 1667 production, but *The Masque of the Two Devils* in Act II was substantially expanded. In 1667 it had been sung by two devils and four allegorical figures in three sequences each separated by interjections from the mortals. In Shadwell's *Tempest* there is an extra devil, and an extra sequence of singing. Furthermore the content of each sequence of singing is considerably expanded. All the modifications serve to intensify the terror as the supernaturals upbraid Alonzo, Antonio and Gonzalo with their crimes of usurpation. After the apparitions have vanished, Shadwell, as if

	Shakespeare	1667	1674
Come unto these yellow sands	I, ii: Ariel	II: Ariel	III, i: Ariel
Full fathom five	I, ii: Ariel	II: Ariel	III, i: Milcha
While you here do snoring lie	II, i: Ariel	—	—
The Masque of the Devils	—	II	II, iii
Arise, arise! ye subterranean winds	—	—	II, iii: Devil
I shall no more to sea	II, ii: Stephano	II: Trincalo	II, i: Trincalo
The master, the swabber	II, ii: Stephano	II: Trincalo	II, i: Trincalo
No more dams I'll make for fish	II, ii: Caliban	II: Caliban	II, i: Caliban
Flout 'em and cout 'em	III, ii: Stephano	—	—
Dry those eyes	—	II: Ariel	III, iii: Ariel and Milcha
Go thy way	—	III: Ferdinand, Ariel	III, iii: Ferdinand, Ariel
The Masque of Iris, Ceres and Juno	IV, i	—	—
We want Musick, we want Mirth	—	IV: Caliban	IV, ii: Caliban
The Masque of Neptune	—	—	V
Where the bee sucks	V, i: Ariel	V: Ariel	V: Ariel and other sprites

FIGURE 7   Vocal numbers in *The Tempest*

revelling in his macabre invention, brings back one devil who sings the thundering new song *Arise, arise! ye subterranean winds*. This 'horrid Masque', as Gonzalo describes it, wrings from the mortals entreaties for mercy and cries of penitence, and thus it plays a significant part in the unfolding of the plot.

The most substantial addition is *The Masque of Neptune* in Act V in which the gods give their sanction to the resolution of tensions by ensuring the mortals a peaceful and entertaining journey home. Singing, dancing, and machines unite in a sumptuous spectacle at which Gonzalo exclaims 'This Art doth much exceed all humane skill.' As it begins,

Neptune and Amphitrite, Oceanus and Tethys rise out of the Sea in a Chariot drawn with Sea-horses: on each side of the Chariot, Sea-gods, and Goddesses, Tritons and Nereides[8]

and three elaborate episodes of singing and dancing follow.

In addition to the vocal music, the new production of *The Tempest* included eleven four-part string movements newly composed by Matthew Locke. These substantial introduction and inter-act 'tunes' strongly reflect the influence of contemporary French theatre music, and ideally complement the French inclination of the remainder of the production. Other dances and incidental music were composed, probably by Draghi, but these have not survived.

John Downes drew a clear distinction between the earlier *Tempest* 'before 'twas made into an Opera', and Shadwell's, which he specifically described as 'an Opera' by virtue of its 'having all New in it; as Scenes; Machines'.[9] The scene he particularly remembered over thirty years later was the end of Act V 'Painted with *Myriads* of *Ariel* Spirits', and the machines he described in most enthusiastic detail were those of the Apparitions' feast in Act III scene iii. Both scenes considerably expanded their counterparts in the 1667 production, and were designed to demonstrate mechanical marvels. Locke also described *The Tempest* of 1674 as an opera on the grounds that although it contained the spoken dialogue demanded by English theatrical taste, it was composed 'with Art . . . in such kinds of Musick as the Subject requires' and with 'splendid Scenes and Machines to Illustrate the Grand Design'.[10]

The musical resources of *The Tempest* were as lavish as the production. The rubric at the head of the quarto text of the play specifies that 'the Band of 24 Violins, with the Harpsicals and Theorbo's which accompany the Voices, are plac'd between the Pit and the Stage'. As in the Chapel Royal, not all members of the band would have played at one time, but it is significant that for this spectacular new production, the King made a section of his band available. Shadwell's epilogue specified that over thirty singers were involved in the production, and an entry in the Lord Chamberlain's records dated 16 May 1674 confirms that these included men and boys from the Chapel Royal released specifically by the wish of the King.

Chappellmen for the theatre.

It is his Majesty's pleasure that Mr. Turner and Mr. Hart or any other men or boys belonging to his Majesty's Chappell Royall that sing in the Tempest at His Royal Highnesse Theatre doe remaine in towne all the weeke (dureing his Majesty's absence from Whitehall [at Windsor]) to performe that service ...[11]

The Tempest of 1674 was the most sumptuous production that the Restoration stage had seen to date, and music played a crucial role in its grand design (Fig. 8).[12] The Duke's Company secured the services not only of the finest performers of the day, but also of the foremost composers. Locke's eleven inter-act movements are the most diverse and ambitious music of their kind yet written for the English stage.[13] They also represent Locke's most sustained commitment to the French style, and four of them are named dances which appropriate the finer subtleties of contemporary French dance measures. However, they transcend French models in the richness of their musical textures which include 'Counterpoint ... Fuge, Canon, and Chromatick Musick',[14] and these, according to Locke, distinguish his inter-act music from that of any possible rival.

Locke's movements achieve an idiosyncratic reconciliation between instrumental idioms derived from French theatrical practice on one hand, and his own instinctive contrapuntal interaction of all four parts, his gaunt melodic lines, and their consequential palette of restless chromatic harmony on the other. This, together with the variety of textures and often violent changes of mood, lends these movements a propulsive vitality that is often absent from the string movements of his church music. The most innovative movement is the Curtain Tune introducing Act I, a vivid piece of illustrative music which suggests a placid sea

The First Musick
    Introduction   Locke
    Galliard   Locke
    Gavot   Locke

The Second Musick
    Sarabrand   Locke
    Lilk   Locke

Act I
    Curtain Tune   Locke
    The First Act Tune: Rustick Air   Locke

Act II
    I shall no more to sea   *?
    The Master, the Swabber, the Gunner,
       and I   *?
    No more Dams I'll make for fish   *?
    A flourish of Musick   *?
    The Masque of the Three Devils   Humfrey
    Arise, arise! ye subterranean winds   Reggio
    Dance of the Winds   *?Draghi
    The Second Act Tune: Minoit   Locke

Act III
    Come unto these yellow sands   Banister
    Full fathom five   Banister
    Dry those eyes   Banister
    Dance of fantastick Spirits   *?Draghi
    Go thy way   Banister
    The Third Act Tune: Corant   Locke

Act IV
    We want Musick, we want Mirth   *?
    The Fourth Act Tune: A Martial Jigge Locke

Act V
    Musick playing on the Rocks   *?
    The Masque of Neptune   Humfrey
    Tritons' Dances   *?Draghi
    Where the bee sucks   Humfrey
    The Conclusion: A Canon 4 in 2   Locke

    *Music not extant

FIGURE 8   The Music in *The Tempest* 1674

developing into the tempestuous storm which is raging as the action begins. Locke's graphic illustration is achieved through powerful contrasts of prevailing rhythmic values ranging from minims to demisemiquavers, and by extremes of pitch range taking his bass instruments down to low B″ flats at the climax in bar 25. These contrasts are complemented by changes of dynamics which Locke specified in the score, 'soft', 'lowder by degrees', 'violent', 'lowd', and finally 'soft and slow by degrees'. Purcell may well have had this movement in mind when he wrote the Dance of the Furies in Act II of *Dioclesian*; he may similarly have remembered Locke's Lilk when writing the Hornpipe in the First Music of *The Fairy Queen*, and Locke's canonic Conclusion when providing a similar canon 4 in 2 as the Dance for the Followers of Night in Act II of *The Fairy Queen*.

The most extensive vocal music in the 1674 production of *The Tempest*, and of comparable weight to Locke's instrumental movements, were the two masques newly composed by Pelham Humfrey. Although he had been back in England for over six years and had not written any other theatre music of similar proportions, Humfrey nevertheless brought to their composition an idiosyncratic amalgam of the Anglo–Italianate dramatic style most familiar from the work of Locke, and idioms absorbed from Lully's *comédies-ballets* of the mid-1660s.

The Masque of the Three Devils in Act II strongly reflects the style of *comédies-ballets* like *L'Amour médecin* (1665), *La pastorale comique* (1667), and *Le Sicilien* (1667), any one of which Humfrey may have seen in Paris. These alternated spoken dialogue, instrumental movements, and vocal numbers all of which were unified by a recognizable dramatic thread. Their solo vocal numbers are predominantly in triple time with occasional interpolations of duple-time phrases of more declamatory recitative. Triple-time textures range from the lyrical to the dance-derived and even the declamatory. Their ensembles are usually in three homophonic parts, are in triple time, and are compounded of short, simple phrases and frequent cadences; these were often danced.

The solo sections of Humfrey's first masque are predominantly in this French hybrid triple style, and they are occasionally punctuated by phrases in duple time. The most declamatory episode is in triple time, and is assigned to the first devil at the beginning of the second of its four vocal sequences (Ex. 50). It is accompanied by an almost static harmonic foundation, and as the

Ex. 50

50.34

First devil: Ty - rants, by whom your subjects bleed, Should in pains all o -thers ex - ceed;

Second devil: And bar - ba-rous mon-archs who their neigh - bours in - vade, And their crowns un - just - ly would get;

second devil resumes a more lyrical manner, the bass line becomes progressively more active. This recitative in triple time is exceptional, and Humfrey's triple-time solo writing is predominantly in the simple dance-related style commonly found in his songs. The most prominent episodes in duple time accompany two of the four allegorical characters in the fourth sequence of singing (50.121–9), but in this masque contrast of metre is not employed with any consistency to delineate character or dramatic situation. Each of the vocal sequences concludes with a short three-part homophonic ensemble, and all but the last are in triple time after the French manner. There is no sense of any calculated tonal organization in this masque.

In *The Masque of Neptune* in Act V, Humfrey adopts the more familiar Anglo-Italian conventions of Locke, and manipulates them with greater dramatic assurance and impact. The masque falls into three sequences of singing, each separated by a dance whose music has not survived. The masque has an overall ternary tonal design, and its three sequences have tonal centres of G minor, B flat major, and G minor respectively. Humfrey appropriates the Italian convention whereby the action unfolds in declamation in duple time, and the resolution of tensions is celebrated in lyrical lines in triple time. The first two sequences are almost entirely in duple time except for the short duet for Neptune and Amphitrite anticipating the return of calm in the first (51.24–39), and the middle section of Aeolus's tripartite song, the centrepiece of the second sequence (51.81–93). In his declamatory lines, Humfrey employed an Italianate melodic mannerism where an anticipatory dissonance leaps to its resolution unexpectedly up a third. He had used this only twice before, and both instances are in his childhood anthems (see Ex. 32), but it is found in *The Masque of the Three Devils* once (50.74), and no fewer than eight times in *The Masque of Neptune* (Ex. 51). The expressive flexibility that Humfrey can compress into a short episode is aptly illustrated in the first sequence, where Neptune sings first imperiously of his subordinate sea-gods in arpeggios and arresting rhythms, and then of the calm that will descend, in mellifluous conjunct phrases with expressive chromatic notes and rests (Ex. 52).

The third and final sequence of the masque (51.107) is entirely in triple time as first each of the principal gods and then each of the subordinates assures the mortals a peaceful return home, and a happy future. The solo lines are predominantly lyrical, and similar

51.72

Aeolus
a

Come down my blus-te-rers swell no more, Your

bc

74

stor - my rage give o'er.

bc

to many of those in the triple-time songs. Each of the sequences of singing concludes with a short, three-part homophonic ensemble that was to be danced, and which reverts to the French style that is otherwise absent from this masque.

Each of the masques concludes with a separate song. *Arise, arise! ye subterranean winds* at the end of *The Masque of the Three Devils* was set by Pietro Reggio, a Genoese baritone who wrote a number of songs for the London stage, some of which, including this song, were published in *Songs set by Signior Pietro Reggio* (1680). Reggio is the least celebrated of the composers who contributed to *The Tempest* (1674), and he was probably invited to compose this single song through the influence of Shadwell of whom he was both friend and music teacher. His song is ambitious, and sustains a commanding control through powerful declamation as the devil summons the fury of the elements. *The Masque of Neptune* concludes with Humfrey's elegant and unpretentious setting of *Where the bee sucks*. Unlike any other songs in *The Tempest*, it is bipartite, and its triple section changes the mode from A minor to A major. Humfrey's only other song to change

Ex. 52
51.17

Neptune
b

Te-thys, no furrows now shall wear, O-ce-a-nus, no

19

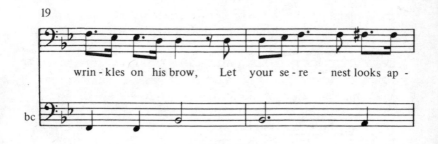

wrin-kles on his brow, Let your se-re-nest looks ap-

21

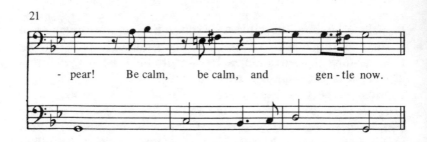

-pear! Be calm, be calm, and gen-tle now.

the mode thus is his second setting of *How well doth this harmonious meeting prove* (32b), and this suggests that the latter may also date from the end of his life.

Banister's four songs in Act III are all simple lyrics, and each is built from pairs of regular balancing phrases. The echo song, a canonic dialogue between Ferdinand and Ariel, is musically simplistic, but obviously made a memorable impression in the theatre. Banister's four songs, together with Humfrey's *Where the bee sucks*, were published on two additional folios paginated 77–80, and entitled 'The Ariel's Songs in the Play call'd *The Tempest*' that

Playford inserted into some copies of *Choice Ayres, Songs, &*
Dialogues (1675).[15] At the foot of the final page, he added the
melody of an additional song, James Hart's *Adieu to the pleasures*
entitled 'Dorinda Lamenting the loss of her Amintas'. Despite the
absence of this text from either printed text of the play, the
inclusion of the song here has prompted some commentators to
propose that it was nevertheless part of the production. It is rather
more likely that Playford, recognizing that he had a small space
remaining, included the melody of a song by one of the singers in
the production, particularly as it was sung by a shepherdess who
shared her name with one of the new characters in *The Tempest*.
Playford included the song complete with bass line, and with no
mention of *The Tempest*, in the next edition of *Choice Ayres, Songs,*
& Dialogues (1676).

By all accounts *The Tempest* of 1674 was a popular success, and
according to Downes 'not any succeeding Opera got more Money'.
Only a small number of performances were recorded, but its
popularity is confirmed by the production of a parody by the
King's Company, *The Mock-Tempest; or, The Enchanted Castle*.
This was the work of Thomas Duffett, and opened at the rival
house in Drury Lane on 19 November 1674. The impact of the
original is further attested in the music of *The Tempest* which has
been attributed to Purcell.[16] The Masque in Act II of the later
Tempest contains two prominent episodes for two devils in the
hybrid triple-time, declamatory-lyrical French style of Humfrey's
Masque of the Three Devils, a style that otherwise remained almost
without influence in England. The first phrases of each masque
disclose a distinct similarity of melodic contour and harmonic
structure (Ex. 53). There is an even closer affinity between the two
masques in Act V where Humfrey's setting of the phrase 'To your
prisons below' finds a striking resonance in the setting of the same
text beginning the middle section of Aeolus's aria *Come down my*
blusterers (Ex. 54).

Although Humfrey's finest work lies most consistently in his
verse anthems, the music he wrote for *The Tempest* at the end of
his life demonstrates that he could create an idiosyncratic synthesis
of French, Italian, and English styles in his theatre music as
distinctively as he had done in the church music. The outcome
may not have been as fine or as influential in the long run as the
church music, but it does make an essential contribution to the
picture of the vitally flourishing artistic environment that grew up

Ex. 53(i)   Humfrey

Where does the black Fiend Am - bi - tion re - side, With the mis - chie-vous De - vil of Pride?

(ii)   ? Purcell

Where does the black fiend Am - bi - tion re - side, with the mis - chie - vous De - vil of Pride?

Ex. 54(i)   Humfrey

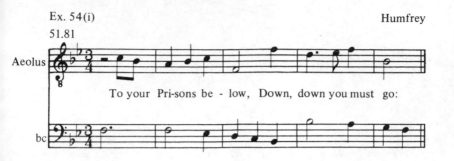

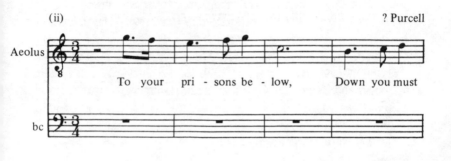

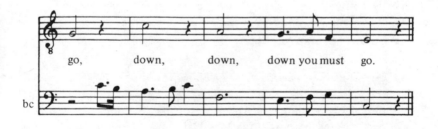

in the first fifteen years of the Restoration. Humfrey was one of the most gifted products of this environment, and his contributions played a crucial part in consolidating a distinctively English baroque style, and in bringing it to the peak of excellence it achieved in the generation immediately prior to the age of Purcell.

NOTES

CHAPTER I

1 *Roger North on Music*, ed. John Wilson (London, 1959), p. 350.

2 *The Diary of Samuel Pepys*, ed. Robert Latham and William Matthews (London, 1970–83), 23 April 1661.

3 Kenneth Cooper and Julius Zsako, 'Georg Muffat's Observations on the Lully Style of Performance', *Musical Quarterly*, liii (1967), p. 244.

4 *Calendar of State Papers Domestic Series*, 1661.

5 Ibid., 1662. See also *The King's Musick*, ed. H. C. De Lafontaine (London, 1909; repr. New York, 1973), pp. 159–60.

6 Cooper and Zsako, 'Georg Muffat's Observations', p. 224.

7 John Playford, *A Brief Introduction to the Skill of Musick* (London, 1664), p. 91.

8 *GB-Lbl* Harleian MS 7338, f. 2ᵛ.

9 Ibid., f. 3.

10 Ibid., f. 2ᵛ.

11 De Lafontaine, *The King's Musick*, pp. 237 and 243.

12 *GB-Lbl* Harleian MS 6346.

13 *GB-Ob* Rawl. MS poet. 23.

14 De Lafontaine, *The King's Musick*, pp. 305–7.

15 J. L. Chester (ed.), 'The Marriage, Baptismal and Burial Registers of the Collegiate Church or Abbey of St Peter, Westminster', *Harleian Society*, x (1876), p. 184; and John Hawkins, *A General History of the Science and Practice of Music*, 5 vols. (London, 1776), iv, p. 428.

16 William Boyce (ed.), *Cathedral Music*, 3 vols. (London, 1760–73), iii, p. x.

17 E. F. Rimbault, *The Old Cheque-Book or Book of Remembrance of the Chapel Royal from 1561 to 1744* (London, 1872), p. 213.

18 Boyce, *Cathedral Music*, ii (1768), p. viii.

19 Cooper and Zsako, 'Georg Muffat's Observations', pp. 223–32.

20 Robert Veel, *New Court-Songs, and Poems* (London, 1672), pp. 106–7.

21 De Lafontaine, *The King's Musick*, pp. 246 and 247.

22 Ibid., p. 254.

23 Ibid., p. 263.

24 Original will no. 553, Archives Department, City of Westminster Public Library. Reproduced and discussed in Peter Dennison, 'The Will of Pelham Humfrey', *Royal Musical Association Research Chronicle*, vii, p. 25; reproduced in *The New Grove*, viii, p. 778.

25 Henry Keepe, *Monumenta Westmonasteriensia* (London, 1682), p. 360.

26 John Playford (ed.), *Choice Ayres and Songs* (London, 1681), pp. 49–50.

27 Henry Purcell, *Orpheus Britannicus*, i, 3rd edn (London: Pearson, 1721), p. vi.

CHAPTER II

1 *Roger North on Music*, ed. John Wilson (London, 1959), p. 291.

2 *GB-Lbl* Egerton MS 2960.

3 William Child, *The First Set of Psalmes of III Voyces* (London, 1639), title page.

4 Evelyn, *Diary*, ed. E. S. de Beer (Oxford, 1955), 28 October 1654.

5 Pepys, *Diary*, ed. Robert Latham and William Matthews (London, 1970–83), 27 July 1661, 21 December 1663.

6 John Playford, *A Brief Introduction To the Skill of Musick* (London, 1664), p. 76.

7 Pepys, *Diary*, 13 February 1667, 14 September 1662.

8 *GB-Bu* MS 5001, p. 118.

9 *GB-Lbl* Add. MS 31437, ff. 29–43.

10 Matthew Locke, *Anthems and Motets*, ed. Peter le Huray, *Musica Britannica*, xxxviii (London, Stainer and Bell, 1976). Discussed in Peter Dennison, 'The Sacred Music of Matthew Locke', *Music & Letters*, lx (1979), pp. 60–75.

11 *Musica Britannica*, xxxviii, p. 108. The inclusion of this verbal text naming Locke as its composer in James Clifford's *The Divine Services and Anthems*, 2nd edition (London, 1664), p. 399, proves this anthem to have been composed by 1664 beyond reasonable doubt.

12 *Œuvres complètes de J.-B. Lully: Ballets*, i, ed. André Tessier (repr. New York, Broude, 1966), p. 43.

13 *GB-Och* MS 1183, f. 103ᵛ; *The King's Musick*, ed. H. C. De Lafontaine (London, 1909; repr. New York, 1973), p. 161.

14 *Œuvres complètes de J.-B. Lully: Motets*, i, ed. Felix Raugel (repr. New York, Broude, 1966), p. v.

15 Ibid.

CHAPTER III

1 Charles Burney, *A General History of Music*, 4 vols. (London, 1776–89), iii, p. 445n.

2 The outlines of this progression are present in Ex. 7, bars 4–5 by Banister; however it lacks the distinctive chromatic alteration.

CHAPTER IV

1 The single source of this anthem, *GB-Bu* MS 5001, p. 179, is the only autograph of a complete anthem by Humfrey to have survived. In the same composite collection, there is an instrumental movement in D major (pp. 157–8) in Humfrey's hand in a style quite unlike that of any of his known works. It immediately precedes Cooke's anthem *We will rejoice* which is in another (?Cooke's) hand, is also in D major, and which otherwise lacks a prelude. Neither has any thematic affinity, but Cooke's initial preludes were independent of the following material. I would conjecture that this movement is the prelude composed by Cooke for *We will rejoice*, and written out here by Humfrey.

2 *GB-Och* MS 53, p. 121.

3 *US-R* Vault M2040 A628, p. 103.

4 *Anthems and Motets*, ed. Peter le Huray, *Musica Britannica*, xxxviii (London, 1976), p. 89.

5 *GB-Cfm* MS 117, f.141ᵛ.

6 *Œuvres complètes de J.-B. Lully: Motets*, i, ed. Felix Raugel (repr. New York, Broude, 1966), p. 60.

7 *GB-Lbl* Add. MS 17784, f. 177ᵛ.

CHAPTER V

1 For a complete chronology, and an account of the origins of the ode, see Rosamond McGuinness, *English Court Odes 1660–1820* (Oxford, 1971), pp. 1–15.

2 The texts of both are included in Robert Veel, *New Court-Songs, and*

Poems (London, 1672). The date 1672 for *See mighty Sir* is given in Veel's index, and 'Sung to the KING *on his Birthday* 1672' prefaces *When from his throne* in Veel's collection, p. 94.

CHAPTER VI

1 For a broad discussion of early Restoration secular song, see Ian Spink, *English Song, Dowland to Purcell* (London, 1974), pp. 151–200.

2 *Roger North on Music*, ed. John Wilson (London, 1959), p. 350.

3 Both are in *Westminster-Drollery*, I (London, 1671), pp. 1 and 2.

4 See *The London Stage 1660–1800. Part I: 1660–1700*, ed. William Van Lennep, Emmett L. Avery, and Arthur H. Scouten (Carbondale, 1965), p. 180. All dates of entertainments at court, and productions in the city are derived from this source.

5 Veel, *New Court-Songs, and Poems* (London, 1672), p. 119.

6 John Playford, *Choice Ayres & Songs* (1679), p. 57.

7 *GB-Lbl* Add. MS 14399, ff. 7 and 14^v.

8 See Spink, *English Song*, p. 156.

9 Extracts from each section are found in Spink, *English Song*, p. 162.

10 Extracts from each section are found in Spink, *English Song*, p. 187.

11 *GB-Och* MS 49, p. 109.

CHAPTER VII

1 Preface to *Andromède*, reprinted in Henry Prunières, *L'Opéra italien en France avant Lulli* (Paris, 1913), pp. 326–7.

2 'A Jigg called Macbeth' arranged, in its earliest source, for cittern in Playford's *Musick's Delight on the Cithren* (1666), and 'The Witches Dance' *GB-Lbl* Egerton MS 2957, f. 5^v. For the complex history of the music for *Macbeth*, see Roger Fiske, 'The "Macbeth" Music', *Music & Letters*, xlv (1964), pp. 114–25.

3 Reprinted in Allardyce Nicoll, *A History of Restoration Drama* (Cambridge, CUP, 1952), p. 173.

4 Curtis A. Price, *Henry Purcell and the London Stage* (Cambridge, 1984), pp. 7–11.

5 See *The London Stage 1660–1800. Part I: 1660–1700*, ed. William Van Lennep, Emmett L. Avery, and Arthur H. Scouten (Carbondale,

1965), p. 215. This date is determined by circumstantial evidence, but it could not have been immediately earlier as the singers and instrumentalists who were members of the Royal household had spent six days around 23 April at Windsor for the annual St George's Day celebrations.

6 John Downes, *Rosicus Anglicanus* (London, 1708), p. 34. Some doubt has recently been cast on Shadwell's sole responsibility for the adaptation, but no substantiation is offered. See George Robert Guffey, *After The Tempest* (Los Angeles, Augustan Reprint Society, 1969), p. ix. But see also G. Thorn-Drury, 'Some Notes on Dryden', *Review of English Studies*, i (1925), pp. 327–30. I am grateful to Dr Curtis Price for drawing my attention to these studies, and to those cited in notes 7 and 13.

7 *GB-Lbl* Egerton MS 2623, f. 55. Pierre Danchin has questioned whether this Epilogue is by Shadwell. See Pierre Danchin, *The Prologues and Epilogues of the Restoration 1660–1700, Part I*, ii (Publications Université Nancy, 1981), p. 593.

8 This rubric is found in the second literary text, *Songs and Masques in The Tempest*, which is reproduced in facsimile and discussed in J. G. McManaway (ed.), 'Songs and Masques in *The Tempest* [c. 1674]', *Theatre Miscellany, Luttrell Society Reprint*, xiv (1953), pp. 71–96.

9 Downes, *Rosicus Anglicanus*, pp. 33–5.

10 Matthew Lock[e], *The English Opera* (London, 1675), Preface.

11 *The King's Musick*, ed. H. C. De Lafontaine (London, 1909; repr. New York, 1973), p. 271.

12 Modern edition of the complete music by Michael Tilmouth, *Locke: Dramatic Music, Musica Britannica*, li (London, 1986).

13 Modern edition by Peter Dennison in *Matthew Locke: Incidental Music, The Tempest, Musica da Camera*, xli (London, OUP, 1977). The first three 'tunes' are ascribed to Robert Smyth in a seventeenth-century instrumental bass part now in *US-NH*, Filmer MS 7, ff. 23^v–24. In a copy of *The English Opera* also in the Yale Music Library, the first three 'tunes' are marked with a cross in a ?contemporary hand. See Robert Ford, 'The Filmer Manuscripts: a Handlist', *Notes*, xxxiv (1978), pp. 814–25.

14 *The English Opera*, Preface.

15 The copy in the Bodleian Library, Oxford contains the additional folios.

16 Edited by E. J. Dent, *Purcell Society Edition*, xix (London, 1912).

LIST OF WORKS

CHURCH MUSIC

1	Almighty God who mad'st thy blessed son
2	By the waters of Babylon
3	Haste thee O God
4a	Have mercy upon me O God, first working
4b	Have mercy upon me O God, second working
5	Hear my crying O God
6	Hear my prayer O God
7	Hear O heav'ns
8	I will always give thanks (the 'Club' anthem, with William Turner and John Blow)
9	Lift up your heads
10	Like as the hart
11	Lord teach us to number our days
12	O be joyful
13	O give thanks unto the Lord
14	O Lord my God
15	O praise the Lord
16	Rejoice in the Lord O ye righteous
17	The king shall rejoice
18	Thou art my king O God
19	Service in E minor (morning, communion, and evening)
20	Chant in C

COURT ODES

21	See mighty Sir
22	Smile smile again
23	When from his throne

SECULAR SONGS

24	Ah fading joy
25	A lover I'm born and a lover I'll be
26	As freezing fountains

all verse anthems composed by 1664

Bow down thine ear
It is a good thing to give thanks
The heavens declare the glory of God
The Lord declared his salvation

MODERN EDITIONS

Numbers 1–12 in Peter Dennison (ed.), *Humfrey: Complete Church Music: I, Musica Britannica*, xxxiv (London, Stainer and Bell, 1972).

Numbers 13–20 in Peter Dennison (ed.), *Humfrey: Complete Church Music: II, Musica Britannica*, xxxv (London, Stainer and Bell, second, revised edition, 1985).

Numbers 46–9 in Peter Dennison (ed.), *Pelham Humfrey: Complete Solo Devotional Songs* (Sevenoaks, Novello, 1974).

Numbers 50–2 in Michael Tilmouth (ed.), *Locke: Dramatic Music, Musica Britannica*, li (London, Stainer and Bell, 1986).

Note on Have mercy upon me O God (4a)

As *Pelham Humfrey* reaches the final stages of production, Robert Ford's article 'Henman, Humfrey and "Have mercy"' has been published in the *Musical Times*, cxxvii (August 1986), pp. 463–6. Ford makes a plausible case that the first working of *Have mercy upon me O God* (4a) is not a childhood anthem by Humfrey, but one modelled on Humfrey's more familiar setting (4b) by Richard Henman over a decade after Humfrey's death. His case fails, however, to account for the strong circumstantial evidence of Pepys in 1663 (see page 6) linking the setting in question with the youthful Humfrey. Pepys identifies the text, the scoring for five voices, and the fact that the composer was one of Cooke's boys. All this points strongly to Humfrey, the most prominent of the chorister composers, and his authorship is strengthened further by its sharing of musical material with the later working (4b). The copy text of the earlier working (*GB-Lbl* Add. 30932) has been proved by Ford to be in Henman's hand, and Henman's initials are clearly at the end of the anthem, but in the light of the alternative evidence I find it difficult to go on to conclude that Henman was not only copyist but composer despite the later word of James Hawkins.

P.J.D.

SELECT BIBLIOGRAPHY

De Lafontaine, H. C. (ed.), *The King's Musick* (London, 1909; repr. New York, Da Capo, 1973).

Dennison, Peter, 'The Life and Work of Pelham Humfrey', 2 vols., including a critical edition of the complete music (unpub. diss., University of Oxford, 1970).

——, '[Purcell:] The Stylistic Origins of the Early Church Music', *Essays on Opera and English Music* (Oxford, Blackwell, 1975), pp. 44–61.

Dixon, Graham, *Carissimi* (Oxford, OUP, 1986).

Evelyn, John, *Diary*, 5 vols. ed. E. S. de Beer (Oxford, Clarendon, 1955).

McGuinness, Rosamond, *English Court Odes 1660–1820* (Oxford, Clarendon, 1971).

North, Roger, *Roger North on Music*, ed. John Wilson (London, Novello, 1959).

Pepys, Samuel, *The Diary of Samuel Pepys*, 11 vols. ed. Robert Latham and William Matthews (London, Bell, 1970–83).

Price, Curtis A., *Henry Purcell and the London Stage* (Cambridge, CUP, 1984).

Rimbault, Edward F., *The Old Cheque-Book or Book of Remembrance of the Chapel Royal from 1561 to 1744* (London, 1872; repr. New York, Da Capo, 1966).

Spink, Ian, *English Song, Dowland to Purcell* (London, Batsford, 1974).

Van Lennep, William, Emmett L. Avery, and Arthur H. Scouten (eds.), *The London Stage 1660–1800. Part I: 1660–1700* (Carbondale, Southern Illinois University Press, 1965).

INDEX OF WORKS